RE-SETTLEMENT OF EX-SERVICEMEN IN INDIA

RE-SETTLEMENT OF EX-SERVICEMEN IN INDIA

Problems, Patterns and Prospects

SATYENDRA KISHORE

CONCEPT PUBLISHING COMPANY, NEW DELHI 110059

The Indian Council of Social Science Research gave the financial support towards the publication of this work. However, the responsibility for the contents of the book — facts, opinions, conclusions, etc. — is entirely that of the author and not of the ICSSR.

ISBN 81-7022-356-3

First Published 1991

Published and Printed by
Ashok Kumar Mittal
Concept Publishing Company
A/15-16, Commercial Block, Mohan Garden
NEW DELHI 110059 (India)

Lasertypeset by
Microtech Advance Printing Systems (Pvt.) Ltd.
H-13, Bali Nagar
NEW DELHI 110015

Dedicated
to the fond memory of
Jayanti Didi

PREFACE

THE SCOURGE of unemployment is at its peak. Industrialisation no longer remains the prime indicator of development. The focus of development has now shifted to ensuring full employment to improve the quality of life of people. Without meeting the elementary needs of health, housing and education of teeming millions, the term 'development' cannot convey its full meaning.

The requirements of elementary needs of the people of Third World countries could be ideally realised by efficient organisation and proper use of their human resources. This confirms the increasing role of academicians in general and social scientists in particular in working out strategies for development. The professional ethics of social scientists have made them better equipped to address themselves to the issues relating to fast transforming and complex realities of Indian society which has painfully sub-humanised its vast majority. It is the need of the hour that sociologists now seek relevance of their academic endeavour in directly relating their output in resolution of a specific contemporaneous or eventual social problem.

The relevance of analytical sociological research remains much more than ever before. The growing annoyance of intellectuals and their vociferous objection to the prevailing inequity, inefficiency and retardation are also reflections of their genuine urge to bring about change in society. The complexities of problems of developing societies, however, demand more closer partnership of social scientists in the prognosis and resolution of emerging social problems. Social scientists are now more urgently required to show specific ways to form a more equitable and just society enabling its vast majority to meet at least their elementary needs of human living.

Between survival and disembarkation of elementary needs of life, there are a number of patterned ways of collective suffering, compromise and compensation. Resettlement is one of the patterned ways of compensating collective deprivation. Conversely, resettlement has also been viewed as a collective process of deferred gratification in developing societies.

The present work has a twin focus : (a) analyses of resettlement of the ex-servicemen as a problem of diagnostic and prognostic inquiry, and (b) understanding the pattern of resettlement in general, including several social categories other than the ex-servicemen.

This book is a pruned and partially modified version of my doctoral thesis submitted to Centre for the Study of Social Systems (CSSS), School of Social Sciences (SSS), Jawaharlal Nehru University (JNU), New Delhi in 1988. A modest beginning was made towards the end of 1983. Initially, an exploratory study was contemplated. In the meanwhile, 'the Government of India, appointed a High Level Committee for going into the problems of ex-servicemen on the 10th March, 1984, which submitted its report on the 27th October, 1984. The perusal of the report entailed reformulating research design and a beginning was made once again in mid-1985.

The study, at least up to the last quarter of 1987, was largely an exercise in inductive research. All theories and frameworks were given up. Emphasis was laid on the collection of empirical facts. Once much of information seeking and its classification was over, the framework and generalisations spontaneously surfaced.

What I expected out of the study in the beginning was nothing more than an opaque empirical work. I never expected that my exploration into somewhat obscure but important subject-matter of research will lead me to a new area of research in Sociology which has been termed as *Sociology of Re-Settlement.*

A 're-settlement study', as it has been indicated in this book, has multi-disciplinary dimensions. Admittedly, therefore, this book has only a limited exposition on the subject matter. Even so, if it has prepared a ground for further multi-disciplinary research on the present area of research, the purpose of my modest attempt is well served.

I am indebted to Prof. T.K. Oommen, who supervised the doctoral work. Prof. Oommen has been specially kind towards me as he took keen interest in the progress of the work despite his busy schedule, particularly due to the added responsibility of Secretary General XI World Sociological Congress, 1986. His incisive reflections and perusal of the draft thesis greatly enriched the work. I wish to express my gratitude to Prof. Oommen for his able guidance and abiding kindness.

My studentship at CSSS/SSS, JNU, also provided me with opportunities to have many fruitful and long deliberations on the problems of resettlement with some of the eminent sociologists, namely, Professors B.R. Chauhan, Y.B. Damle and Yogendra Singh. I am indeed grateful to them for their continued moral support. I am also grateful to Prof. Namwar Singh for his reflexion on my interpretations of Bhikari Thakur's work and also for lending me a book on the subject from his personal library.

During my tenure as a Ph.D. student, we lived frugally as fellowship provided by the University Grants Commission remained the only source of regular income. When my petition for the grant of extension of fellowship for the fifth year had already gathered enough dust, I was served with a notice in July 1988 to immediately vacate my university accommodation at Mahanadi Hostel. The traumatic blow came unexpectedly, at a crucial juncture when I was finalising my draft-thesis. Prof. Ravindra K. Jain, then the Chairman, CSSS/SSS, was kind enough to write two recommendatory letters for me (a) for the extension of fellowship and (b) for grant of my stay at Mahanadi Hostel till the task was accomplished. The letters bore fruit and threatened retardation was set into motion. I am grateful to Prof. Ravindra K. Jain for his kindness and continued encouragement which mitigated my anxiety in a critical phase of my life, enabling me to fulfil my research objectives.

I wish to express my thanks to the officers of Directorate General of Resettlement, Kendriya Sainik Board and All-India Ex-Services League, New Delhi; Rajya Sainik Boards, Bihar and Haryana; Zilla Sainik Boards Patna, Ranchi, Gurgaon and Sonepat; District Treasury Offices, Patna and Ranchi; District Pension Offices, Gurgaon and Sonepat; Security and Intelligence Services, Patna for their cooperation and support in conducting the fieldwork. I feel pleasure in acknowledging with thanks the kind cooperation extended to my by Gen. V.K. Avasthy, the then Director General of Resettlement, Ministry of Defence, Government of India, New Delhi. Brig. Ravi Kumar and Maj. H.S. Noor of Bihar Regimental Centre, Danapur Cantt. made my fieldwork enlightening and comfortable, for which I express my most sincere thanks to them. Thanks are also due to Mr. Alok Kumar Srivastava, IAS, for helping me in the completion of fieldwork of Mander and Khunti blocks in Ranchi district and also for making my stay at Ranchi comfortable. I wish I had placed on record the individuals contribution of inestimable value of all my respondents. Nevertheless, I wish to express my gratitude to all my respondents without their avid interest and generous cooperation the task would never have been complete.

I also wish to thankfully acknowledge the valueable help of Mr. Muralidhar of the Computer Centre, SSS, JNU in the analysis of field data which was extensively used in my doctoral thesis in tabular form. The data of doctoral thesis are now being presented in graphic form for which I received very friendly assistance from Mr. Gaurav Kisan for which I thank him very much.

I am thankful to the Indian Council of Social Sciences Research, New Delhi, for providing financial grant towards publication of the work. The publishers of this book, Concept Publishing Company, extended warm cooperation in various manner in prompt publication of the work without compromising with its quality. I am indeed grateful to the publishers, particularly Messers Naurang Rai, Ashok Kumar Mittal and Alok Kumar Mittal.

March 3, 1991 SATYENDRA KISHORE

CONTENTS

LIST OF TABLES

LIST OF FIGURES

ABBREVIATIONS

AIXL	:	All-India Ex-Services League
BSF	:	Border Security Force
CISF	:	Central Industrial Security Force
CDS	:	Combined Defence Services Examinations
DGR	:	Directorate General of Re-settlement, Ministry of Defence, Government of India, New Delhi
DGET	:	Directorate General of Employment and Training, New Delhi
EBR	:	Evenly Balanced Re-settlement
Emp.	:	Employed
FCI	:	Fertilizer Corporation of India
FR	:	Formal Re-settlement
GOI	:	Government of India
HFC	:	Hindustan Fertilizer Corporation
HLC	:	Report of the High Level Committee on Problems of Ex-servicemen, Government of India, 1984.
INA	:	Indian National Army
IMA	:	Indian Military Academy
IRDP	:	Integrated Rural Development Programme
JCO	:	Junior Commissioned Officer
KSB	:	Kendriya Sainik Board
MT	:	Motor
NCO	:	Non-Commissioned Officer
NDA	:	National Defence Academy
NFL	:	National Fertilizer Limited
NFR	:	Non-formal Re-settlement
OR	:	Other Ranks (Includes J.C.Os)
OTC	:	Officer's Training Camp

RCF	:	Rashtriya Chemical Fertilizer
RPF	:	Railway Protection Force
RSB	:	Rajya Sainik Board
RSS	:	Rashtriya Swayamsevak Sangh
SC	:	Scheduled Castes
SE	:	Self-Employed
SSI	:	Small Scale Industry
ST	:	Scheduled Tribes
UP	:	Uttar Pradesh
USI	:	United Services Institution
XSM	:	Ex-servicemen
ZSB	:	Zilla Sainik Board

1

INTRODUCTION

THE EMERGENCE of welfare state, primarily as a consequence of industrial revolution, witnessed the state being gradually forced to take up the responsibilities of well-being of its citizen. Often the pressure put on the State manifests itself through various popular movements and the State response is articulated through legislations. Ensuring full employment to its people has now become one of the major welfare objectives of every State irrespective of its nature or type. The Directive Principle of State Policy of Indian Constitution declares providing full employment to all its citizens as one of the State's most important goals. The goal so far has hardly been realised. No single sociological or economic explanation can be sought for the persistence of mass-unemployment which looms large as a major political issue impinging on countless socio-political unrests since Independence. No doubt, with the slow but impressive agricultural transformation, gradual accelerating industrialisation and large-scale deliberate expansion in services; there has been marked increase in number of vacancies and the employment potentials have increased multi-fold. But the generation of seemingly vast employment potentials has always fallen short of the number of persons wanting jobs primarily because of the fast multiplying population and tremendous growth in educated manpower. The gap between the number of vacancies available and persons wanting job is ever widening since Independence.

The need for re-settlement of ex-servicemen arises primarily because there is greater supply of manpower in practically every sector of our economy than the vacancies available. In a hypothetically reversed situation, a discussion on the re-settlement of ex-servicemen may appear meaningless and most of the functions of the Directorate of Re-settlement, Ministry of Defence, Government of India (henceforth being referred to as DGR), may become redundant. Therefore, re-settlement of ex-servicemen can best be conceived as a process of making special effort[1] by the State to help the ex-servicemen re-settle in their post-retirement life, which essentially means making adequate arrangements for their re-employment or self-employment by various means and ensuring their smooth placement in the civilian occupational system. Viewed this way, a re-settlement study should mainly attempt to make a systematic understanding of interaction between the special provisions made by the State for the re-settlement of a particular group or group responses to the provisions made as well as their responses to the problem itself.

Basic Premises

The entire process of re-settlement begins with the following four basic premises:

1. That most of the ex-servicemen retire early and for survival they invariably require a job soon after retirement.
2. That there is no favourable sign in the overall economic scenario which may narrow down the gap between the number of persons wanting jobs and the numbers vacancies available in

the foreseeable future.

3. That prolonged military training and uniform service conditions, coupled with their impressive and ever-increasing numerical strength, set ex-servicemen as a category apart, which for several reasons, deserves and requires special treatment of the State.
4. And, finally, that the compulsions of the nature of job in the services are such that most of the ranks have to retire between the 32-41 age group and the government is incapable of guaranteeing them a job up to 58 by lateral placement or otherwise, which may be comparable to the civilian job tenure - and the State, pursuing the policy of mixed economy, expects positive contributions from the private sectors, associations and ex-servicemen themselves, for the amelioration of their problems.

Justification of the Problem

A scientific understanding of 'the development and nature and laws of human society' has been one of the primary sociological concerns from the early days of the emergence of this discipline.[2] This primary concern of sociologists has rendered the study of social problems under severe criticism, though the study of social problems is not formally excluded from the subject-matter of sociology. Despite its 'slashing' criticism, sociology in many countries is said to have been 'fathered' by the study of social problems.[3] More respectable treatment to the study of social problems is given by our sister discipline, social work,[4] because of their explicit "conviction that rational and scientific solutions to social problems could be found through social reform and individual guidance".[5] Nevertheless, as specialists in research methodology, it is argued that some sociologists made contributions of inestimable value to administrators of social agencies who desired scientific appraisals of the effectiveness of their welfare programmes. In fact, for more than half a century sociologists and social workers have co-operated closely in a wide variety of activities designed for community betterment. Thus, so far as scientific understanding of the social problem is concerned, sociological concepts and theories and, to a great extent, their methods and techniques can provide the best answers.

An attempt, therefore, is being made to make a scientific understanding of the problems of ex-servicemen in general which essentially revolves around their re-settlement. The choice of the problem is indeed guided by its 'topicality, currency and pragmatic derivations'.[6] As already suggested, considering professional socialisation of the past, the uniformity of rank they hold even after retirement, statutory provisions controlling and regulating their post-retirement behaviour, uniformity of pensions, economic status and, by and large, similarity of the problems that they face in general make the ex-servicemen a highly distinct social category. The population of this special social category is rapidly increasing. It is estimated that now 65,000 to 70,000 are being added every year to the existing population of around 3 million ex-servicemen. The early age of retirement, added family responsibilities, gradual disintegration of old system of social security based on village kinship, caste and joint family system and virtual absence of modern social security system make their problems more acute than a qualified young job-seeker. An average ex-serviceman finds himself in a paradoxical situation of competing at once with retired civilians and fresh job-seekers with hardly anyone of his age to compete and throw a challenge.

Re-settlement is a process, which not only endeavours at smooth second-career transition but also attempts to bear the jerks of transition itself by way of institutional counselling, guidance, training and liaisoning. There is close and intimate inter-play between the institutions controlling, regulating and assisting the ex-servicemen and the objective realities of the society to which he returns. Competition, caste, family, rank, status and a variety of other social factors start constraining him soon after he gets released from the services. Both 'resettlement' as a process and problem and 'ex-servicemen' as a significant social category are important in our contemporary national context – hence the justification of the present problem of research.

As a part of introduction, we now intend to dwell upon the concept of re-settlement in some greater detail. This exercise is necessary at least for two reasons. First, that it is the first word of the title of the present work, therefore, the word must be adequately exemplified so that our deliberations in the subsequent chapters may have clear and definite meaning. Second, that in India the term 're-settlement' is being applied for a variety of social problems and processes. Therefore, it is also worthwhile to examine whether the term "re-settlement" has a definite meaning when it is applied to different contexts and categories.

The terms 're-settlement' and 'rehabilitation' are at times confused and used interchangeably. Further, the meaning of the term re-settlement cannot be fully appreciated without understanding the term "settlement" since in the former the meaning of the latter is subsumed. While discussing the terms settlement, re-settlement and rehabilitation, we do not intend to establish a continuum among the three. They are indeed three distinct sociological processes. But a simultaneous discussion of the three at one place exemplifies the meaning of each of the three related concepts and particularly that of re-settlement which concerns us for the moment.

Settlement, Re-settlement and Rehabilitation

Re-settlement pre-supposes dislocation from settlement. Etymologically, of numerous meanings given,[7] we have preferred the term settlement to mean 'establishment in life, in an office or employment' for the purpose of the present analysis. Viewed this way, settlement refers to a process of status acquisition in society and creation of interests in the relationship which surround one. Settlement, therefore, is a universal process depending upon one's ascribed/achieved status and personal ability and interests.

The nature of settlement, however, differs from society to society in terms of those undertaking primary responsibility of settlement of an individual. For example, a man of a status or ascriptive society gets settled in his life as per his ascribed status and the prevalent norms of his tribe, caste or estate. It is the responsibility of elders in the family, kinship, tribe or caste to see that the growing child properly acquires occupational skills of the family and on attaining adulthood he shares rights and duties of every economic activity of the family like any other member. In typical achievement-oriented societies, however, the individual concerned is solely responsible for his settlement. The questions of major decisions pertaining to the choices of job, life partner, etc., are to be resolved by the individual concerned. In matter of one's settlement an individual has to proceed almost in unaided manner; parents usually taking up the responsibility of schooling them only up to high school stage.

A brief reference on the concept of 'settlement' exemplifies the term "re-settlement". Re-settlement as a process has a very restricted meaning. It limits itself only to the sociological aspects of seeking a second or subsequent career after putting in a major part of one's economically productive life to a given employment/self-employment. The crucial aspect in defining the process of re-settlement is that it is not an end result of an individual's own choice, he is compelled by the requirements of his job to leave it at an age when he would have rather preferred to continue in the job. Thus, it is not changing jobs as is the case with the managerial class, white collar technical hands and floating industrial workers, etc., in Indian situation. The waiting period from one job to another for such class may be termed as a stage of 'frictional unemployment' or 'transit period for professional mobility' or 'preferred voluntary unemployment' for a short period. This is apparently done to enhance one's skill to find better job prospects which are also often clubbed with attending to numerous personal items which remain unattended because of the professional compulsions and the rigours of an industrial society. Thus, with the concept of re-settlement a sense of compulsion is associated for those requiring it explicitly or implicitly. If anyone refuses to be in employment or opts out of work, he is out of purview of the present study. We will subsequently notice that it is in this sense that those who voluntarily opt out of the services are excluded from the definition of ex-servicemen.

Rehabilitation,[8] on the other hand, is a related process for which the victim himself is not responsible. An individual being subjected to rehabilitation is a child of circumstances. One can cite numerous examples - a victim of war, riot, flood, famine, fire, or landslide, earthquake, cyclone, etc., or deformed birth having permanent mental or physical impairment or delinquency, etc., to name only a few. Thus, those who need physical, mental, economic or social rehabilitation, seldom consent to the misfortune and peril which surround them.

The special nature of the problems of ex-servicemen in the contemporary socio-economic framework necessitates "re-settlement" as an alternative for mitigating their problems. As it has already been defined, re-settlement is a process by which some additional support is ensured to the interested parties who are themselves anxious to sort out their problems and are prepared to take up the challenges by exploiting the additional support - whether by formal institutions/associations or by the informal sources. Definitionally, in the process of re-settlement, it is presumed that the person concerned will take the first initiative and seek the additional support extended or assured. On the other hand, where rehabilitative measures are required, the State machinery and other welfare associations/organisations are obliged to go to the door-step of victims to extend their support and give relief to the party of rehabilitation, whether an individual or a group among such victims want such relief or not. Thus, in rehabilitative measures, it is the catastrophe and its victims which are important. It is the collectivity or the aggregate connected with an unforeseen and uncontrollable calamity which is important for taking up any rehabilitative measure rather than an individual. In case of the subjects of re-settlement this is not so. They are treated as an end-product of some unavoidable socio-economic process which consigns them to some unfavourable and deprived position. The subjects of re-settlement are treated individually rather than collectively by the State machinery and other institutions for the purpose of extending any relief. The relief granted is not generalised in nature, as is in case of rehabilitative measures. Every one intending to get re-settled institutionally must take his first initiative to successfully claim the extra support being provided by the Government in their favour.

TABLE 1.1: Showing Those Responsible for Taking Decision and Making Efforts for Tackling the Situation/ Problems of Settlement, Re-settlement and Rehabilitation

Problems/ Processes	Responsibility in terms of degree of desirability		
	Primary responsibility	Secondary responsibility	Preferred Responsibility (no formal responsibility)
Settlement	Individual	Family, relations & peer groups	State
Re-settlement	Mutual, the victim (individual) and those responsible for his deprived state of affairs (institution)	Family, relations & peer groups	Either *only* the victim or only those responsible for his state of affairs
Rehabilitation	Societal, Governmental	Family, relations & peer groups	Individual

If settlement, re-settlement and rehabilitation are the three sociological processes which must take place when conditions for any one of them exists, the question then arises as to who should take up the primary and overall responsibility for initiating the process to resolving the problem. In other words, if conditions of any of the three processes exist, who should be expected to come forward and provide relief? For the performance of a great number of social functions, an individual is socially recognised to be primarily responsible. In other words, it is the duty of the individual to take appropriate measures in a given circumstance, viz., in case of settlement. Similarly, it is the primary responsibility of the State and other welfare organisations to take up rehabilitative measures if situations so warrant. It is in this sense that the process of re-settlement falls in-between settlement and rehabilitation, as re-settlement measures are supposed to be taken up on mutual basis, both by the individual and the State. Therefore, Table 1.1 provides a schematic view in terms of those generally found responsible for taking decision and making necessary arrangements for the three processes.

Usually settlement has individualistic personal reference - it concerns an individual and his very personal matters. Whereas both re-settlement and rehabilitation have group reference, viz., re-settlement or rehabilitation of an individual of such and such group. Similarly, in terms of temporal orientation, settlement always has futuristic reference whereas both re-settlement and rehabilitation have past reference. In case of re-settlement and rehabilitative measures, the cause of action arises due to certain deprivation or calamity already occurred to the victims of either of the two processes, respectively. Thus, in case of re-settlement and rehabilitation the temporal orientation must have a past reference. This is not the case with the process of settlement. It depends upon the ambitions of the individual, what he expects and wants to achieve in his career. It is in this sense that 'settlement' has futuristic orientation. The temporal, social and spatial references of the problems of settlement, re-settlement and rehabilitation can be viewed from Table 1.2.

TABLE 1.2: Showing the Temporal, Social and Spatial References of the Process/Problems of Settlement, Re-settlement and Rehabilitation

Reference	Problem/Process		
	Settlement	Re-settlement	Rehabilitation
Temporal	Future	Past	Past
Social	Individual	Group	Group
Spatial	Disperse	Localised	Localised

Thus, settlement always refers to an individual and is always oriented towards future which is spatially dispersed in the universe, whereas both re-settlement and rehabilitation have group reference, past orientation and localised spatial framework.

Because of their greater similarities, the terms re-settlement and rehabilitation have been quite often used inter-changeably. Still, as it has already been discerned there lies a clear difference between the two concepts in terms of the responsibilities attributed to tackle or mitigate the problem in individual cases. Those who are subjects of the rehabilitation of any type are not expected to take initiative for tackling their problems. Whereas, in the case of re-settlement both the subjects of re-settlement and those primarily responsible for the conditions of such subjects are to share the responsibilities in tackling their problems. It is considered joint responsibility and it is this sense of jointness of responsibilities which delineates the term from settlement, on the one hand, and rehabilitation, on the other.

The joint responsibility of re-settlement may be shared with an individual member either by a formal institution, usually the one which caused him to get out of work prematurely, or by the primary relatives of the sufferer.

The Matter of Re-settlement

The matter of re-settlement is compensation for the deprivations incurred throughout one's occupational career. The need for such compensation may be explicitly recognised by the State or implicitly conceived by the society. The deprivations, thus recognised or conceived, are primarily economic and socio-psychological. The politically deprived groups, as mentioned already, require a compensation of different order which we have named as rehabilitation. And further, re-settlement as a compensatory process is applicable only to the occupational categories having like experiences of deprivations with reference to other majority occupations with comparable status. The numbers of occupational categories thus deprived must find themselves in minority among the set of comparable occupations in a given political economy.

The process of re-settlement, therefore, emerges out of the explicit or implicit concern for compensation of an occupational group having economic and/or socio-psychological deprivation conditioned by its nature of work and the economic and socio-psychological rewards associated with it. The sense of deprivations gets sharpened when the objective conditions of work and reward system associated with it are considered as "minority occupations" and are compared with the "like majority occupation" enjoying the same social status but having better economic and socio-psychological rewards. The following six factors contribute to the emergence of re-settlement as a compensatory process for the members of any occupational category who are considered as deprived, merely as a result of such factors, either 'jointly' or 'severally':

1. Conditions requiring separate living of a worker from his family (especially that of procreation) for the most part of his occupational career. Such conditions may prevail (a) either because of the low and/or precarious income associated with an employment or self-employment or (b) because of the tough organisational norms, for example, those of the military and para-military forces requiring its rank to live in the barracks with their colleagues in non-family stations depriving them for the most part of their career to live with their families. Resettlement, therefore, pertains to all those who emigrate to some distant place to seek job or gainful occupation but are compelled, by way of paucity of funds or the requirements of the job, to maintain their family somewhere else (usually the native place) than the place of work. The one who becomes a subject-matter of re-settlement has a history of maintaining his family (particularly of procreation) from a distant place by way of regular remittances and only by infrequent personal care materialising through occasional visits on important occasions or long leave.

   Those who are unable to live with their family by virtue of low and precarious income and high cost of living of the cities include the unskilled urban/'industrial workers' from the villages or petty self-employed unorganised workers such as those vending milk, eggs, fish, vegetable, fruits and other such consumer items which chiefly belong to the informal sector.

While explaining the conditions requiring a worker to maintain his family from a distance, it is assumed that all those, who migrate to urban centres and industrial towns from their respective villages in search of some gainful employment or work or join the armed forces, are first men and, secondly, such men love to live with their respective families as part of their self-fulfilment and meeting their most basic socio-psychological needs. It follows, therefore, that all those who are constrained to keep their family members in the vicinity of their place of work must consider themselves as deprived to the extent they are obliged to carry the burden of maintaining their respective families from a physically unapproachable distance. Thus, an economically well-placed person having capacity to keep his wife and children with him but voluntarily chooses to keep them at his native place or somewhere else on personal considerations, does not fulfil the requirements of the conditions of re-settlement and therefore is excluded from its definition. It is being emphasised here that re-settlement applies only to those who are constrained or inhibited to keep their families where they work. Therefore, re-settlement is applicable only in those cases where external compulsion or forbearance is sufficient enough to preclude a working hand from keeping his family with him at the place where he had to live for working.

2. The second condition is the physical requirement of the job leading to early retirement. The examples include all such careers conditions by such physical requirements as those working in the armed

forces, outdoor sportsmen, circus workers, etc. The air-hostesses and sportswomen and lady circus players in certain cases may have identical physical requirements of early retirement but are taken here as exceptions and excluded for the purpose of the present formulations. Similarly, among the outdoor sports, highly paid sports, like cricket, tennis, etc., are excluded which compensate its career incumbent adequately enough before they are physically unable to play and also because the players of such games generally come from the high echelon of society providing them better standards of socio-economic securities than the other sportsmen, viz., hockey, football, basketball players, athletes, wrestlers, swimmers, etc., in the Indian context.

3. The third important condition is the number and intensity of socio-economic obligations left to be performed directly as consequence of conditions (1) and (2) mentioned above either jointly or separately. In case of ex-servicemen, all the three conditions are met, viz., they have to work away from their family for the most part of their career; the requirements of their job make them to retire early and, finally, which is also crucial in as much as that a great many of their socio-economic obligations, such as education, marriage and employment of the children, etc., yet remain to be fulfilled. Although the migrant labourers and the outdoor sportsmen are the exclusive examples of (1) and (2) above, respectively, for majority of them their socio-economic obligations remain to be fulfilled and, therefore, are among those who require re-settlement measures.
4. The fourth important condition is that income from the previous career (employment or

self-employment) allows negligible or only scant savings so that when he returns home to live permanently he finds his pension or savings quite meagre and inadequate to face his obligations and responsibilities. Therefore, he must be under compelling need to supplement his income by hook or by crook. By previous career it is assumed that those working in a career roughly for a decade or more will only be included for the purpose of the present analysis.

5. The fifth condition is the numerical preponderance of those conditioned by the above four factors, whether occupationally or territorially. Therefore, individual cases or socially insignificant numbers will not qualify themselves to become a subject-matter of the present study.
6. And finally, the group claiming or being considered as a subject- matter of re-settlement must have its historicity whether occupationally or territorially. The occupations or territories giving rise to the conditions 1 to 5 above must have a history of at least two or more generations. Therefore, the occupationally deprived category of first generation in its occupational history will be excluded for the purpose of our analysis.

Re-settlement as a Social Process

Settlement is applicable to all societies irrespective of stages of development. It is expected of a child in every society that once he grows up he will create a world of his own and thereby become responsible for all that he does in his personal matters. He is expected to satiate his basic needs from the nest that he weaves and in the very process of weaving he undertakes a number of economic activities. The recognition of the fact of an individual being responsible to the woman he marries and the children he procreates is the starting point of the concept of settlement. Thus, settlement is a process to meet the socially recognised requirement to satiate one's primary needs in and through his family and rights and duties emerging from such recognition. It is in the realm of duties, responsibilities or obligations towards one's family that most of the activities of settlement are guided.

With the duty to take care is associated the right to earn reasonable livelihood. In the under-developed simple societies, rights and duties are mutually complementary. Family, kinship, caste and other social institutions unfailingly help an individual to meet his family obligations the moment he establishes or is made to establish his family. In developing (transitional) societies, the duty to take care remains, but the social institutions, such as family, kinship, caste, etc., turn insipid in securing an 'individual' the right to earn his reasonable livelihood. It is now expected of the State to ensure reasonable livelihood to its every citizen but the State finds itself incapable to meet such demands. In developed societies, too, duty to take care of one's family rests with the head of the household but the State in such societies is well capable of ensuring the rights of an individual to earn his reasonable livelihood.

Similarly, in every society there is a prescribed time period in which one must do certain kind of activities during one's life span.[9] In the process, various institutions interact with an individual member of a society. In the under-developed societies, family, kinship, caste, religion and other social institutions ensure that an individual does what he is expected to do in a given age group. In developed societies, social institutions lose their efficacy in ensuring the performance of socially prescribed roles of a given age-set. The role is taken over by economic institutions and State legislations.

Table 1.3 clearly shows that the socially recognised duties and rights correspond in developed (complex) and under-developed (simple) societies. In developing transitional societies, however, whereas the socially recognised duties exist, there is absence of corresponding rights of the citizen.

TABLE 1.3: Showing Occurrence of Socially Recognised Duties and Corresponding Rights by Types of Society

Types of society	Socially recognised duties	Corresponding rights
Under-developed (Simple)	+	+
Developing (Transitional)	+	-
Developed (Complex)	+	+

This is not to equate simple societies with technologically and economically developed/complex societies. The two are indeed different. But when they are viewed in terms of socially recognised duties and corresponding rights, there is complementary relationship between the two in both types of society. The historical and anthropological evidences show that, in simple society, social institutions take care to ensure a reasonable livelihood for an individual. In all developed societies, the same is ensured either by legislative mechanism (example - socialist republic) or by creating favourable economic environment (for example, advanced capitalist countries where demand and supply curves of the labour market show mutually comparable trend). As an example of developing society, the Indian case can be cited where neither the economy is capable of providing work to its teeming millions nor legislative provisions exist to ensure right to work as a fundamental right, a reference of it being only feebly made in Directive Principles of State Policy of our Constitution (Article 41).

The scarcity of resources, whether natural or artificial, in developing societies and the rising expectations of the masses have put extra strain on every segment of a society - the individual, the society and the State. Re-settlement appears as a major social process where all the segments of society find themselves under strain and incapable of performing the functions which they are expected to do. It is, therefore, a process of tension management in developing societies.

Re-settlement, thus conceived, applies to a section of the rural workers of Unorganised Sector (Fig 1.1) of all developing societies who are compelled or lured to seek employment in the organised sector – the income, benefits or service conditions of which force them to maintain their families in the villages and be content with only occasional home visits once in a while. Re-settlement also applies to self-employed workers in the cities drawn from rural areas. Therefore, the petty shopkeeper, wage earners, self-employed skilled/unskilled workers in the cities coming individually or in groups to earn their livelihood in the cities and thereby maintain their families in their respective villages can be viewed as subject-matter of re-settlement. They come from a class which provides them at least some social and economic security on the basis of which the individual migrating worker can leave his family in his village-home. The class of people among the ex-servicemen being dealt with here also belongs to the similar group and therefore, has been chosen as typical category where re-settlement applies.

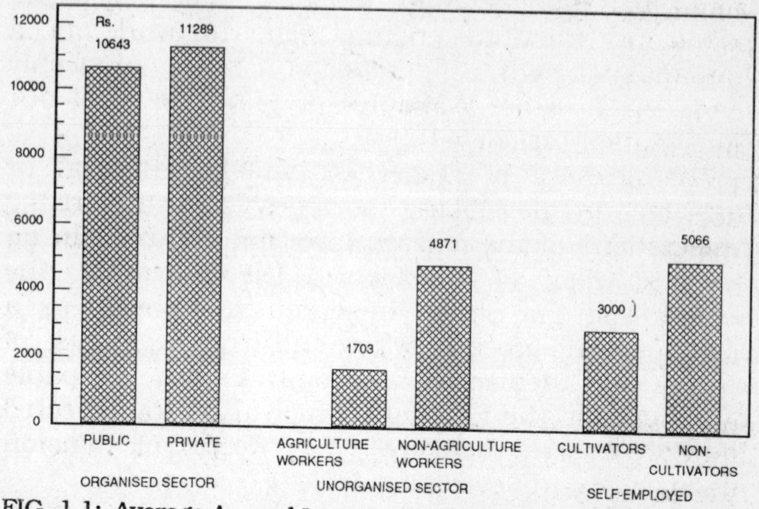

FIG. 1.1: **Average Annual Income Per Worker (In rupees)**[10]

In the under-developed societies, motivation to move out of the villages is less due to lack of job opportunities in the urban areas. Although the urban ward migration of male married workers exists as a major migration process of developing societies, even in the under-developed societies such migration does take place by induction of rural menfolk to the ranks of its army. Then, one may ask a hypothetical question - Does an ex-serviceman of an under-developed society require re-settlement measure? The answer is in the negative as he will not feel deprived once he is retired because he will comprise the ideal reference group for the people among whom he will return to live both socially and economically.

In developed societies, too, re-settlement as a major social process relating to job and career does not exist because of the growth of industrialisation and urbanisation and lack of any surplus labour in the villages which can be used to play a subsidiary role in the cities. Even those working among the ranks in the armed forces enjoy for most of their career living with their respective wives and children. The term of service is longer and after retirement there is no waiting period for the second job, if wanted.

Re-settlement, therefore, finds its existence only in the developing societies as major career processes. In under-developed and developed societies there is only settlement. In the former, mainly because those who can take care of their settlement by way of employment/self-employment of any sort, are a few and, therefore, not considered as deprived in any sense. Even if a few among them require resettlement, the State is incapable of or is not in need of providing institutional arrangements for the re-settlement of any occupational category. In the latter societies, the labour supply is often less than the employment demand generated. Therefore, choice of work depends upon the personal qualities and interests of an individual. The institutional barriers and socio-economic bottlenecks do not require the State here to make special arrangements for the re-settlement of any particular occupational category or the culture system to create special space for those who migrate from the country-side in the hope that they will come back one day to finally settle down there.

Scheme of the Study

In order to appreciate the problems of ex-service personnel, we have tried to understand their status in Indian society through the past. In the second chapter, the panoramic view of soldier's status in society through different stages in our history has been linked to the present. Then, the third chapter is fully devoted to the discussion of the nature of ex-servicemen's problems, their meaning and scope for the present study. The fourth chapter deliberates upon the methods and techniques of the study. The fifth chapter is about the nature of re-settlement of ex-servicemen. The sixth and seventh chapters contain discussion about factors influencing re-settlement of ex-servicemen in India. And, finally, the eighth chapter deals with the prospects of re-settlement as a sociological process as well as a subject-matter of sociological study.

NOTES

1. The effort is special as against the ordinary measures to combat the problem of unemployment in general.
2. Flower & Flower, *Oxford Dictionary of English Language*, 1975, p. 1088.
3. *International Encyclopaedia of the Social Sciences*, Vol. 14, Macmillan Co. & The Free Press, 1968, pp. 453-54.
4. For an illuminating panoramic view of recent trends in professional Social Work, with special reference to India, see Oommen, T.K., *Professional Social Work – As I See It*, Deptt. of Social Work, Jamia Millia Islamia, New Delhi, 1987.
5. *International Encyclopaedia of the Social Sciences* , *op. cit.*, p. 495.
6. *Ibid.*, p.453.
7. Little William, *The Shorter Oxford English Dictionary on Historical Principles*, Oxford, 1968, p. 1956.
8. *Ibid.* See p. 1693. Little explains rehabilitation as:

   "To restore by formal act or declaration (a person degraded or attained) to formal privileges, rank and possessions; to re-establish (a) person's good name or memory by authoritative pronouncement; (b) to re-establish the character or reputation of a person or thing".

   "To restore previous conditions; to set up again in proper condition."
9. For example, Principles of *Ashram Dharma* among Hindus.
10. The Histogram has been adapted from a report by V. Venkatesan in the *Times of India*, Dec. 17, 1990. The report is based on a paper on rural labour entitled 'Even Dogs are Better Off' written by Prof. Jan Breman.

2

SOLDIERS' STATUS IN SOCIETY: An Understanding from the Past

THE EX-SERVICEMEN as a social category are of a very recent origin. The historical evidences suggest that in ancient and medieval periods a person used to be a soldier for life and his recruitment was primarily determined by his ascriptive traits of the *varna* or caste to which he was born. Even in the army of the Company Bahadur the native *sepoys* used to serve the company till the very old age and "those who become unfit for field service, either owing to physical deterioration or age or disability, were allowed to enlist themselves in the 'veterans battalions' which were employed in cities on internal duties".[1]

Although the system of pension and retirement prevailed since the time of Augustus in Roman Army, its evolution in India can be traced only after the revolt of 1857 which were introduced primarily to create and perpetuate a class of loyal natives in society. Besides, it also aimed at attracting young recruits so that their obedient behaviour was ensured either as job-seeker or as an employee and to eliminate all those who continued in service despite being old and inefficient.[2] Initially, those who got retired, though they became veterans or 'ex-servicemen', their problems were basically the problems of retirement and old age. The status of a soldier and his service conditions depended very much upon the nature of society and organisation of the army of a particular period.

It it intended to make here a historical survey of armies and armymen through the ages so that the subject-matter of the present research, as far as it is possible, is also viewed in historical perspective. It is unwise to discount the difficulties and limitations in historical portrayal of the life and work of Indian soldiers which are both evidential and methodological. One can barely cull the information relating to the living conditions of soldiers from the already scant historical material available on the subject. And even if such material were available, problems of comparing the life and work of soldiers in their totality in entirely different contexts will be a very difficult proposition. Finding sociological insights through comparative history in a time series is indeed problematic. Despite difficulties, however, historical trends provide important clues to understand certain contemporary sociological facts and processes to build a tentative rough sketch of a soldier in different periods of our society.

In ancient and medieval societies, the choice of work was determined by the social status of the people. The hierarchy of *varna* and caste and proportionate status associated with each of the *varna* strongly defined the framework within which a person could earn his livelihood in his life-time. Ancient and medieval Indian societies are thus characterised as 'status societies', albeit instances of group or individual mobility are not unknown. However, the pattern and scale of occupational mobility do not go against basic characteristics of 'status society' in which the ascription of a social status determines a person's worth and work rather than personal achievements influencing his social status as is the case in 'class societies'.

With the clustering of *varna* system from the

'second urbanisation' in Northern India from the sixth century B.C., the *Kshatriyas* provided primary recruitment base for different kingdoms. During the beginning of the ancient society, the *Kshatriyas* were supposed to defend the realm, to protect the people and the *Dharma*, 'not to forget a kindness or a hurt', not to back out when challenged to fight or gamble, and in the words of the Great Epic they considered it 'a sin to die in bed'.[3] Sir S. Radhakrishnan writes that "they were the defenders of society from external aggression and internal disorder. The military organisation of the State was entrusted to them. They were in-charge of political arrangements. It was not the intention of the Hindu *Dharma* to make the entire body of people a general levy".[4] Nevertheless, the instances of non-Kshatriyas getting recruited in the army and holding responsible positions are not few even from the very early days of the ancient society.

The Sultanate period in medieval India is characterised by strong foreign element in its nobility, so much so that even the local converts of recent generations, who formed the bulk of the Muslim population, "began to discover for themselves as far as possible a foreign ancestry".[5] The large scale influx of the foreigners like the Afghans, Persians, Mughals, Turks and Uzbeks, etc., and their domineering position in the contemporary Indian politics and society had somehow shaken the well laid down process of self-evaluation and emulation from within *varna* frame of reference. At least a section of them now started seeking foreign ancestry, alliance or allegiance. The new process of 'foreignisation' if one may use the term, was soon to disappear with the Indianisation of the nobility under the Great Mughals.[6] The process of Islamisation[7] went hand in hand with 'foreignisation' and the non-Muslim base of the former got strengthened during the Mughal period. The process of 'foreignisation', albeit for the indigenous Muslims, did transgress the *varna* model of self-evaluation and emulation at least for short spell of about 400 years in our long and varied history.

It was basically as a reaction to the utter perversion of religious orthodoxies and caste rigidities that different regions of the sub-continent started witnessing the *Sufi* and *Bhakti* movements. Sikhism grew primarily as a product of over all *Bhakti*-trend in society, which, towards the close of 16th century, got crystallised as martial race championing the cause of Hindus in general and in turn being viewed by them as rejuvenated Kshatriyas of higher order. It was a paradoxical situation: Sikhism theoretically denied caste distinction but in reality the caste distinction, under the supremacy of Jat Sikhs, persisted. Yet, the entire community was being viewed by the Hindu collective conscience as militant, reformed and rejuvenated Kshatriyas having raised their arms against Aurangzeb to uphold their pride and defend their honour. True, at any given time in the ancient and medieval India, there remained numerous kingdoms and principalities, but all who fought for the armies got subsumed into *varna* fold getting the position of Kshatriyas.

The foregoing paragraphs suggest that in ancient and medieval societies the choice of work was largely determined by one's birth in a particular caste or *varna* or one's association, by descent, to a particular tribe or race. The element of bravery, however, irrespective of one's origin or birth was recognised and the lucky few among them also got rewarded often by their induction into the Kshatriya *varna*.

In ancient and medieval periods, though the warrior class occupied second rank in the social order, next only to the Brahmins, outside *varna* framework, they probably constituted the elite of society. All original sources, directly or indirectly, refer to this fact. Status society, by its very characteristics, seldom left any scope for retirement from the hereditary occupations, except for physical inability or renunciation. Therefore, considering the position of warrior class in ancient and medieval societies, one may state that they lived like aristocrats or at least were highly privileged in society.

It is with the coming of Europeans and, more especially, the East India Company on the Indian socio-economic and political scenes that the traditional framework of society took a new direction; essentially as an overall consequence of economic interest of British colonialism the choice of work now gradually and very slowly became a matter of one's personal abilities and achievements rather than one's birth in a particular religion or caste. It is ironical, however, that although the Indian army was the backbone of the British rule yet the soldiers were the last to get 'modernised' as compared to the emerging new middle classes, such as petty merchants, lawyers, teachers and salaried clerks of the government, railways, post-office and banks, etc. From the early days of East India Company certain revolutionary changes occurred in the organisation of the army – its control and command, financial administration, supply, recruitment and more specially in terms of gun based sophisticated arms ammunition. Still it took about nearly two centuries for the 'undisciplined and indifferently armed guards of peons' of small establishments who "were enrolled with dual object of protecting the factories of the East India Company and lending dignity to its functionaries to become prized soldiers of British Indian Army".[8] A brief outline culled from the leaves of history can tell an interesting story of the making of an Indian soldier which is also considered relevant for the purpose of the present analysis.

In the second half of the 17th century, the British, the Dutch, the French and the Portuguese were the major European contenders competing for commercial supremacy in India. The resolution of differences with the Portuguese on European plane and the defeat of the Dutch at Chinsura (Bengal) in 1759 led the British to concentrate at quelling the French in Southern India. The struggle for supremacy between the French and the British changed the character of peace seeking mercantile companies into military contenders which resulted into the birth of 'the concept of regular army of Indians'. "The origin of the regular native army, however, dates back to 1784, when Stinger Lawrence, the 'Father of the Indian Army', enrolled a native force in Madras."[9]

The victory of British East India Company at the battle of Plassey (1757) and Wandewash (1760), with instrumental support of Native Army, set the British eyes on the decadent Hindu and Muslim States which itself had emerged as a result of the decline and disintegration of the Mughal Empire. Despite the consistent mistrust of the English on their native forces, the economic compulsions and political considerations entailed their gradually growing ascendancy on the Native Army. The number of the Native Army grew by leaps and bounds; only the Bengal Army saw the native troops growing from 24,000 in 1746 to 1,28,000 in 1857-58.[10]

The East India Company did not come to India to raise an army and to conquer the country. It was by sheer chance that the British became the ultimate carrier of the improved instrument of warfare and advanced organisational set up of the west and to take full advantage of it on the politically decadent and socially degenerated soil of the time. The British intrusion and conquest was an adventure of avarice. As no adventure could be carefully planned, the initial growth of the company's army essentially remained accidental and haphazard.

The Presidency armies of Calcutta, Madras and Bombay grew slowly and separately albeit under complete subordination of the civil authority of the company and the British Government. The Presidency armies were considered as discrete 'entities existing to play limited part of suppressing local risings' and 'were considered to counterpoise against one another' in times of armed rebellion or mutinies.[11] The de-centralisation of the army with over all subordination of a uniform civil authority was the need of the hour and it duly served its purpose of establishing and consolidating the mighty British Empire in the East.[12] Although with the passing over of the Company's army to the Crown, a new era of planned military development was ushered, it was not considered expedient to unite the Presidency armies as one until the threat of Russian aggression on North-western Province. The Russian danger precipitated the unification of Indian Army in 1895 from where the army got its true character of fighting external enemies rather than policing its people. The changes of 1895 were to pay great dividends for the British in the First and Second World Wars.

The East India Company brought with itself the elements of brewing modernity of Europe which in itself was a consequence of matured commercialism and the factory system of nascent industrialisation. When the East India Company shifted its ambition from mercantile gain to territorial acquisition, it was interacting with Indian socio-political institutions with sophisticated technology and advanced organisational base. From this point onwards we find an interesting interplay of tradition and modernity, each affecting, and getting affected by the other. In earlier times, as we have witnessed in the foregoing paragraphs, with the influx and surge of foreign tribes in India, we found one tradition (or even traditions) meeting another tradition. If the position of the respective tribe in the given contemporary political framework was superior, the process of 'foreignisation' took place; otherwise it has always been indigenisation which has been the primary social process in respect of foreign tribes coming to this sub-continent.

Under the Company rule a relatively superior institution of army, civil administration, etc., were interacting with the orthodox, caste-ridden and 'degenerated' society. Although the prime motivator of the Company and British rule in India was always the perpetuation of the colonial rule so that they may harvest its fruits continually, it is not difficult to find at the same time philanthropic and reformist elements in the army and administration sincerely wanting improvement in the socio-economic conditions of the masses at whatever cost. Still the rule itself could not be perpetuated without active involvement of the masses in manning the Company's army and administration, though initially at rank and staff levels.

The initial thinking in the company considered the employment of 'Natives' in its army as unsafe but the financial considerations always compelled them to look for the 'Natives' to serve and give honour to their army. This was because the 'natives' were both cheap and efficient.[13] "On arguments of safety, an army consisting of Europeans alone would have been ideal. But considerations of safety clashed with the considerations of economy. Thus, a compromise between finances and the problems of defence was inevitable."[14] Gradually, therefore, a system of army developed consisting of overwhelmingly 'native' ranks and European officers. However, the pattern of recruitment of the 'native' ranks, under the three Presidency armies, greatly differed. The consequences of differential pattern of recruitment and work-conditions of the three Presidency armies are of great sociological importance as a handful of European officers had to manage the 'native' ranks with their superior organisational set up and sophisticated arms. For all these they required deeper sociological insights into the natives' affairs. It is not without adequate reasons that a great number of articles contributed by the European officers of the British army in their *USI Journal* reflect rigorous sociological exercise on caste, religion and culture in India.[15]

The *sepoy* mutiny in Bengal army is taken as one of the direct consequences of the exclusive dominance of the local Brahmins and Rajputs in the army and the European officers' pampering their casteism, commensality and religious orthodoxies and in turn gradually succumbing to it:

> "The Bengal Army, unlike the Madras and Bombay Armies, was always difficult to handle because of the high caste men, Brahmins and Rajputs. On the Bengal establishment, low caste men were completely excluded from the fighting force; they were employed only on menial jobs and were not allowed to mix with caste Hindus. . . . The Bengal army did not become Brahminised by any order of government, but simply through recruiting officers, over a series of years, confining their choice to the tallest, cleanest and most handsom looking men, who were undoubtedly of the high castes. Gradually, they came to predominate, and to exercise their influence to keep away all low caste people; and,

finally, the custom became a rule.[16]

Therefore, "the spirit of exclusiveness in favour of high castes which operated to the full on officers and *sepoys* alike, created an atmosphere of potential mutinies. 'A subserviency of officers generally to the feeling of high castes, which gave them handsome and intelligent men, was appreciated in all its strength by the *sepoys*, played with the fears of Brahminised Colonels.' Thus was the germ of resistance to authority and discipline fostered, and Commanding Officers openly admitted the presence of a power superior to discipline. It was this germ that finally became a cause of the Mutiny."[17]

The *Calcutta Review* once remarked about the composition of the Bengal army: "Our *sepoys* come too much from the same part of the country, Oudh, the lower Doab and upper Behar. There is too much of clanship among them which should be remedied."[18]

Similarly, casteism in the Bengal army was strongly objected to by Sir Charles Nupiers who wrote to the Duke of Wellington on June 15, 1850:

"the last and most important thing which I reckon injurious to the Indian Army is the immense influence given to caste; instead of being discouraged it has been encouraged in the Bengal army. In Bombay army it is discouraged and that army is better ordered than the Bengal Army. In the latter (Bengal army), the Brahmins have been the leaders, in every mutiny. In the last mutiny about pay, and which, I may say, was general throughout the Bengal army, though it appeared in six segments only, all appeared to be governed by Brahmins."[19]

The *sepoy* mutiny of Bengal is usually contrasted with those the Madras and Bombay armies[20] which comprised natives coming from different regions and belonging to practically all castes and religions and the officers consciously discouraged the practice of casteism and religious fanaticism to any extent. Even the Brahmin and Rajput sepoys of the Eastern U.P. and Bihar, employed in Bombay and Madras armies, did not indulge in casteism and religious fanaticism. This helped the growth of a 'secular' orientation in those armies. The foregoing discussion provides historical evidence and strength to the fact that, under the Indian conditions, caste and religion can dilute the secular institutions only if, for some reason or other, men responsible for running such institutions either pamper the 'primordial loyalties' or yield to its pressures.

The inter-personal relationship between the European and the Indians has seldom been cordial because of the ethno-centrism and cultural relativism of the former. The face to face relationship between the native Indians and the Europeans in the Army marked the utter humiliation and subjugation of the former by the latter. Despite the order of the Court of Directors in 1813, prohibiting the officers from maltreating the natives, the inhumane and abusive behaviour of the European officers towards the native ranks seemed to have continued unabated. Even a sepoy of European origin could insult a native officer without fear of punishment of any kind. There was a gulf of difference between the rank to rank pay and allowance of Europeans and their 'native' counterparts and stark difference persisted in terms of their physical conditions of living and the amenities and the benefits provided. The inter-personal relationship of the native sepoys and the English officers has been vividly depicted by

Kaye and Malleson:

> "a *Sipahi* on duty always presented or carried arms to an English officer, but an English soldier suffered a 'native' officer to pass by without a salute. Even an English sergeant commanded native officers of the highest rank. On parade, the English officers made mistakes, used wrong words of command, then threw blame upon the *Sipahis* and reviled them. Even native officers, who had grown grey in the service, were publicly abused by European striplings. On the line of march, native officers were compelled to live in the same tents with common *Sipahis*, and had not, as in the armies of native potentates, elephants or palanquins assigned to them for their conveyance how great so ever the distance which they were obliged to traverse. And if they rode horses or ponies, purchased from their savings, the English officers frowned at them. . . . The concubines of the English gentlemen were better paid than the native officers and their grooms and grass-cutters better than the native soldiers, that English officers could import their *zonanas* the most beautiful women in the country, whilst the natives hardly dared to look at the slave girls."[21]

Despite the fact of the native sepoys inhuman conditions and insulting and provocative behaviour by their English counter parts, the traditional notion of high status of a sepoy in society seemed to have lingered throughout the British period before the echoes of Freedom Movement could move the Indian civilians and armymen alike.

> "In England, an Englishman joining the army was forgotten by his family, it was no great source of

pride to an English family to know that one of its members was serving in the ranks of the army of East India Company. In India it was a thing of great pride to join even the ranks; and the boast of many a family was that generation after generation they had 'eaten the salt' of the Company Bahadur."[22]

A sepoy who was personally thoroughly dissatisfied with his work-conditions and the inhuman behaviour of the English elements in the Army, whether in officer cadres or ranks, one may ask as to how did he receive a high social status from his community and how could they feel proud of a man serving in the Company's army even as sepoy? What possible explanations can be given for this ironical situation?

It is a well known fact that the economic impact of the British rule was very unfavourable on Indian masses. It led to the virtual closure of indigenous cottage and small industries and degeneration of agriculture. The agonies of rising mass unemployment and poverty was too often intensified by frequent droughts and famines[23] without hardly any measure to safeguard the life of men and cattle. The salary of the natives employed in the army must have given great relief to their family members and relatives as an assured income could be expected from the incumbent. Apart from the direct financial gains by way of regular remittances, the family members and their relatives must have got indirect advantages; in terms of safety and security of life and material from the anti-social elements as well as the oppressive local authorities. The managers of the British colonialism have consistently considered the armymen – English or native – as their most chosen and favourite servants. The armymen always received the best out of the worst in an enslaved society. Benefits accruing out of the generalised pampering of the army may have discounted the agonies of racial arrogance and lesser pay and allowances of the natives for the same rank. In addition, in the absence of spontaneous industrialisation, the continuance of Brahminical feudal social ethos pertaining to the profession of arms and loyalties to one's master must have accorded substantial legitimacy to the high prestige and power to those serving the army. With the intensification of the Freedom Struggle from the beginning of the 20th century, and the kind of role played by the Indian Army in the Freedom Struggle, its status got diluted. The sepoy mutinies of the early 40s and the formation of INA by Subhash Chandra Bose contributed a great deal in restoring the prestige of armymen during the period when the nationalist sentiments were at their peak.

NOTES

1. Singh, M.P., *Indian Army under the East India Company*, New Delhi, 1976, p. 234.
2. Saksena, K.M.L., *The Military System of India (1850-1900)*, New Delhi, 1974, p. 213.
3. Majumdar, Bimal Kanti, *The Military System in Ancient India*, Calcutta, 1960, p. 28 ('*supposed*' added).
4. *Ibid.*, pp. 13-14.
5. Ashraf, Kanwar Muhammad, *Life and Conditions of the People of Hindustan*, New Delhi, 1970, p. 107.
6. Athar Ali, M., *The Mughal Nobility under Aurangzeb*, New Delhi, 1970, pp. 7-33.
7. Yogendra Singh, *Modernisation of Indian Tradition*, New Delhi, 1973. Yogendra Singh has used the term 'Islamisation' 'to cover three types of cultural and social mobility in status groups through conversion to Islam. . .' (see p. 73). Conversion to Islam was not a dominant factor in the upward mobility of people of India throughout the Sultanate period. More important factor was one's foreign ancestry. Those who could establish or seek foreign

ancestry got important position in political, economic and social life. Conversion to Islam liberated indigenous low caste population from caste atrocities but did not assure virtual mobility in politico-economic sphere. The only route left for any substantial upward mobility in political and economic life of the early medieval period was through the establishment of one's foreign ancestry. Conversion to Islam was, however, a step forward in that direction because without that the search of foreign ancestry would have been meaningless and association with foreign rulers would have been difficult. It was only through the process of indigenisation of nobility under the Great Mughals that the process of 'Islamisation' carries its full meaning. For the entire Sultanate period the process of 'foreignisation' was a more dominant process of social mobility than 'Islamisation'. The process of 'foreignisation' still exists, though in waning form.

8. Saksena, K.M.L., *op. cit.*, p. 1.
9. *Ibid.*, p. 3.
10. *Ibid.*, pp. 6-12.
11. *Ibid.*, p. 262.
12. The de-centralisation of the army was considered to be the requirement of the conditions which prevailed in those days. 'Unavoidable in the early days of the Company's rule with its separate centres at Bombay, Madras and Calcutta, this system was found so useful that no attempt was made at uniting the three armies in 1796. And when the army was re-organised in 1824, the Court of Directors considered it 'useless' to unite the three armies. Even in 1858, when the armies were transferred to the Crown, the old system of separate armies was allowed to continue in preference to having one army for whole of India. As an army officer has put it, there was 'a political safety' in the division of the Indian Army." See M.P. Singh, *op. cit.*, p. 22.
13. The native army had much more endurance and stamina than the European Army. 'A European was considered fit for service in India for above 12 or 15 years, and a native for 20 to 25 years.' See, Singh, M.P., *op. cit.*, quoted from *Minutes of Evidence*, Q. 1422-23, 13, p. 1, Commons, 35 V of 1832, Evidence of Sir Robert Scot.

    Further on the question of efficiency, Lord William Bentinck remarked that Indian Army was the most expensive and the least efficient in the world. Countering his contentions, Sir C.T, Metcalfe thus wrote: "Is it no proof of efficiency that it has conquered all India? Is it no proof of efficiency that

India is more universally tranquil owing to our Indian army than it even was under any Native Government or Governments we read of? If our Indian army be so in expensive, why do we not employ European troops along to maintain India? Why but because that we could not pay a sufficient number? If our Indian army was so inefficient, why do we incur the expense of making soldiers of the natives? Why do we not entertain the same number of undisciplined people who would cost much less? Why, but because then we should lose the country from the inefficiency of our native force". Quoted from Kaye, J.W., *The Life and Correspondence of Metcalfe*, London 1858, II, 128 by Singh, M.P., *op. cit.*, pp. 56-57.

14. *Ibid.*, p. 93.
15. In course of research, the researcher has gone through all the original volumes of the *USI Journals* from 1871 onwards which lie in a highly neglected condition at USI Library, Kashmir House, New Delhi. An exercise of culling down and systematising sociological literature from the Journal can be an interesting subject matter of a justifiable independent research. In absence of workable xeroxing facility in the library, the researcher was generously permitted to go through the volumes in the library itself. The researcher has a list of interesting sociological titles culled down from the volumes but even these are so voluminous that it would be improper to reproduce them here. However, just by way of example, a piece of writing of G.J.M. Evatt, Surgeon of the Army Department is being reproduced which he wrote in 1877: "Caste is one dead-weight that will for years weigh India down for struggle for progress.In a corps like this, where duties are so particularly and intimately concerned with the European race, caste interferes very much. The mere handling of food of the European would be defilement in the eyes of a high caste Hindoo, and Indian Mohamedanism is so paltry a copy of Mohemets original creed that even the Mussulman in Hindostan is entirely caste ridden.

   . . . The present class of Hospital servants is notably Chamars". See Evatt, G.J.M., *USI* Journal (1877: 6), *Notes on a Native Army Hospital Corps for India*, see p. 115.
16. Singh, M.P., *op. cit.*, p. 157.
17. *Ibid.*, p. 158.
18. Vol. II, 51. Quoted by M.P. Singh, *op. cit.*, p. 155.
19. M.P. Singh, *Ibid.*, pp. 157-8.
20. For details, regarding the composition of natives in Bombay

and Madras Armies, see M.P. Singh, *op. cit.*, pp. 154-7.

21. Quoted by M.P. Singh, *op. cit.*, pp. 235-36, from Malleson (ed.). *Kaye's and Malleson's History on the Indian Mutiny*, London, 1888, pp. 160-61.
22. M.P. Singh, *op. cit.*, p. 234.
23. Mohinuddin Alamgir, *Famine in South Asia: Political Economy of Mass Starvation*, Cambridge, 1987, see Chapter 3 for a detailed analysis on "Indian Famines of the past", pp. 58-76.

3

THE EX-SERVICEMEN AND THEIR PROBLEMS

EX-SERVICEMEN, in a very broad sense, currently refer to all those who served in any of the three forces of the Indian defence for any length of time and continue to live at any given point of time. However, "the need for formally defining the term "ex-servicemen" was felt for the first time after 1965 to ensure that the benefits of the new policy of reservations flow only to the really deserving persons. The definition was first formulated in 1966. Subsequently on 15th December, 1979, the Department of Personnel and Administrative Reforms, Ministry of Home Affairs, in their Notification No.39016/10 Estt(C), defined the term "ex-servicemen" for the purposes of employment as under:

> "Ex-serviceman" means a person who has served in any rank (whether as a combatant or as a non-combatant) in the Armed Forces of the Union, including the Armed Forces of the former Indian States, but excluding the Assam Rifles, Defence Security Corps, General Reserve Engineering Force, Lok Sahayak Sena and Territorial Army for a continuous period of not less than six months after attestation and
>
> (i) has been released, otherwise than at his own request or by way of dismissal or

discharge on account of misconduct or inefficiency or has been transferred to the reserve, pending such release or,

(ii) has to serve for not more than six months for completing the period of service required for becoming entitled to be released or transferred to the reserve as aforesaid, or

(iii) has been released at his own request after completing five years' service in the Armed Forces of the Union."[1]

Clause (iii) above entitles all those who are released from the services on compassionate grounds after completion of five years service, therefore, enabling such retiring personnel to claim all those concessions/facilities/privileges which an ex-serviceman after having rendered 15 years of regular service is entitled to get. The latter contends this and *the Report of the High Level Committee on the Problems of Ex-Servicemen*, Government of India, 1984, (henceforth being referred to as HLC) further adds that "taking advantage of the liberal definition, many educated individuals join the services and seek discharge on completion of five years' service only to take advantage of the further benefits to which the ex-servicemen are entitled." (HLC, 1984, p.17). Accordingly, the HLC responded to a uniform demand "for a stricter definition of the term 'ex-servicemen', to ensure that the benefits now existing and those contemplated would be conferred only on the deserving" and thereby recommending a new definition[2] which excludes provisions of clauses (ii) and (iii) above from its purview and makes it applicable only to the regular pensioners subject to certain provisions. Department of Personnel and Training has now accepted the definition as proposed by the HLC (see Appendix 'A') and it has been clarified by the same vide their OM No.

36034/5/85-Estt. (SCT) dated 14-4-1987 that only those retiring after 1 July, 1987, will be covered under the definition.

Scope of Definition of Ex-Servicemen for the Present Study

An 'ex-serviceman' means a person who has served in any rank *from Sepoy to Subedar Major* in the Regular Army of the Indian Union and who retired from the service after earning his pension. A definition of ex-servicemen thus formulated for the present study excludes several categories from the currently adopted definition of the Government.[3] The purpose of limiting the scope of definition is to make the population under study homogeneous so that findings may be applicable to all falling under the defined category. Any attempt at adopting the Government definition of ex-servicemen *in toto* will not only make the present study unmanageable but it will also change the nature of work.

In our definition of ex-servicemen we have made a distinction between officer and non-officer ex-servicemen and we have included only the latter. It has been so done considering their apparent distinction in terms of their ascribed and achieved status – level of education, age of retirement, quantum of pension and savings, social connections, age and education of the children; consumption pattern, style of living and life attitude, etc. In a nutshell, therefore, the resettlement problems of the ranks and *officer* ex-servicemen are of entirely different kinds if at all the officers can be covered under the definition of resettlement.[4] The problems of *officer* ex-servicemen come closer to the problems of retired civil officers/class in general having common experiences of isolation, fatigue and problems related to health and old age. The details of retired defence personnel (1980-83) are depicted in Fig. 3.1(a) and 3.1(b).

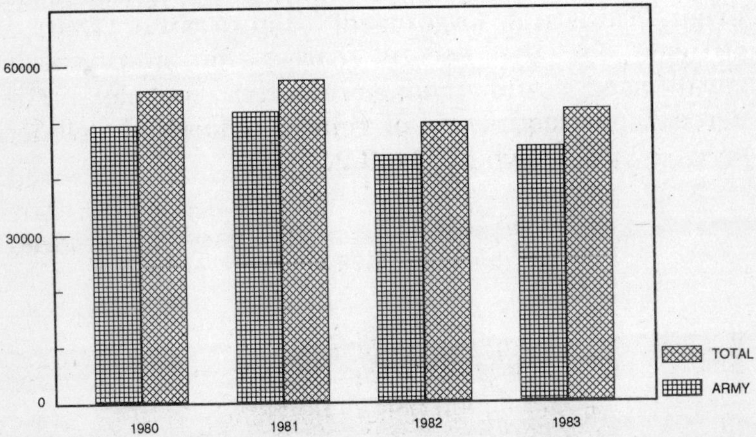

FIG. 3.1(a): Details of Retired Defence Personnel: Other than Officers (1980-83)

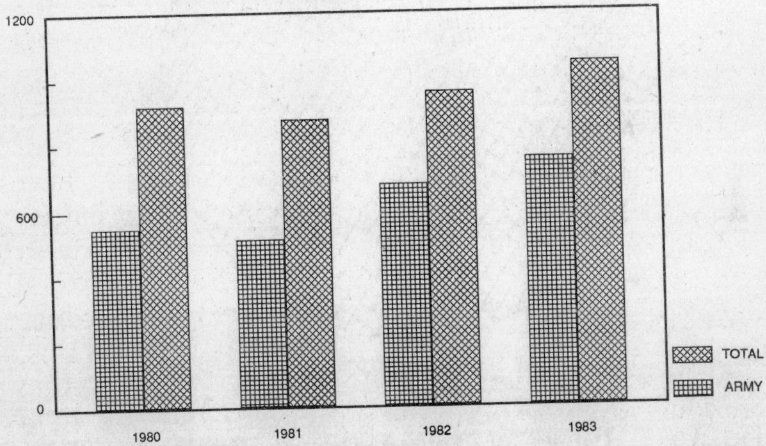

FIG. 3.1(b): Details of Retired Defence Personnel: Officers (1980-83)

The non-officer ex-servicemen of the Indian Navy and Air Force have also been excluded from our definition because most of them acquire fluency in English. They are urban-oriented and also technically qualified enough to get readily absorbed in urban/industrial productive system. For most of them it is a problem of change of job, problem of elimination from the options already available in urban/industrial (organised) sector rather than a struggle for the second career for a primarily rural-based and village-oriented people. The percentage frequnency of retired officers of defence services are shown in Fig. 3.2.

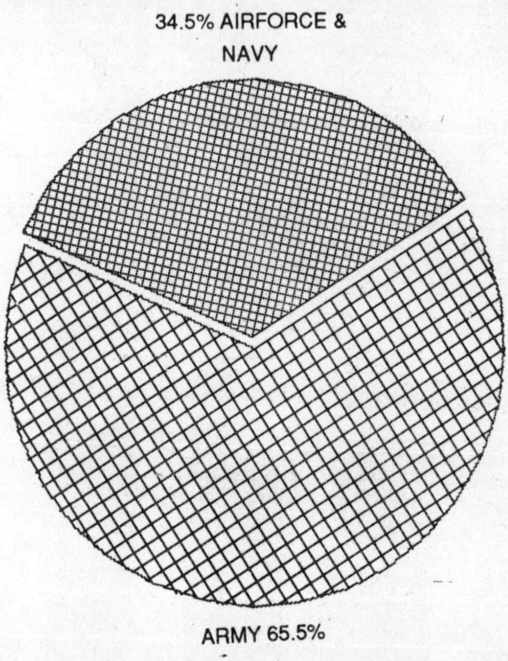

FIG. 3.2: Details of Retired Defence Personnel: Officers Percentage (1980-83)

Physically disabled ex-servicemen have been excluded from our definition because they are the subject-matters of rehabilitation rather than re-settlement as we have already tried to define the two concepts in Chapter 1. Similarly, female personnel too have been excluded from the present definition as they face problems of different kind from those covered under our definition.

However, it may be clarified that the category which has been chosen for the purpose of the present study constitutes around 89 per cent of all ex-servicemen of the three Armed Forces of the Union including the officers as is evident from Fig. 3.3.

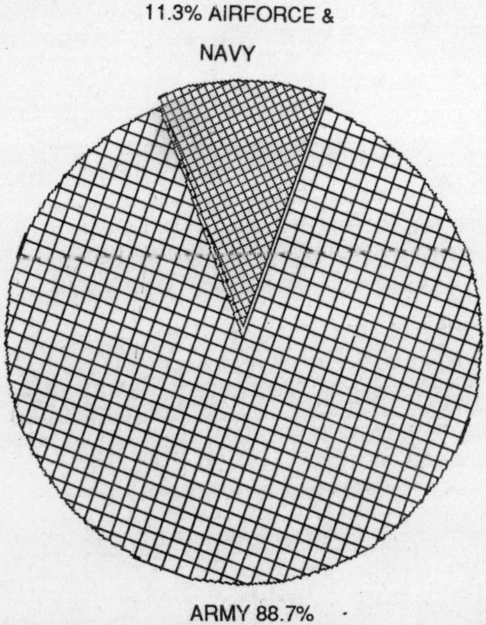

FIG. 3.3: Details of Retired Defence Personnel: Other than Officers Percentage (1980-83)

Therefore, the term ex-serviceman/men hereafter will connote all persons other than officers of Indian Army who retired from the service after earning their pensions. True, the definition also ignores promotee officers retiring as Captain or Major who may have some resemblance of class with the ex-servicemen just defined but they are being taken as exceptions to the rule.

Class, Caste and Ex-Servicemen

The defence services have pyramidic structure and each rank has its own special class characteristics and idiosyncracies. There are as many as 17 ranks in the Indian Army beginning with a young sepoy to the General. The occupant of a particular rank professionally (and, therefore, habitually) considers himself superior to even one rank junior and expects salute and respect from him on every occasion and he is supposed to behave the same before the one who is just one rank above him. Despite the rigid nature of the rank structure, in which the rights and obligations of each rank in respect of its subordinate and superior are minutely defined, they can be broadly classified on the basis of their class characteristics.

Those who come out of the defence services are released from their respective ranks and therefore, tend to retain the class characteristics and idiosyncracies of that particular rank. In terms of rank, there are two major classes:

(i) the Other Ranks (henceforth referred to as ORs) and Junior Commissioned Officers (henceforth referred to as JCOs) and
(ii) the Commissioned Officers.

The ORs and JCOs have traditional social base in society since the Company days. Because till the middle of the 20th century, the officers cadre was predominated by the English, and an Indian could at best aspire to become a Subedar Major. Most of the National Defence Academy (NDA), Indian Military Academy (IMA) and Combined Defence Services (CDS) recruits do not have any traditional basis in the Army and are drawn from the urban middle class background. The recruitment base of the ranks, however, is middle peasantry and families of some of them have traditions of sending their males to the Army for generations in a row.

The ORs and JCOs, in terms of rank, are highly heterogeneous and subordinated. There are as many as seven ranks in this group. For a sepoy, even a Havildar is a very dominating figure – Subedar Major being the virtual king of the ranks and works as a link between the rank and the Commanding Officer. Subedar Major is a coveted position in the Army, entry to which is limited only through promotion from the ranks. While a young recruit aspires to reach one day at this level, he commands a near spontaneous respects from the young Commissioned Officers who are taught by him many secrets of the trade. The ORs and JCOs, therefore, despite having differences among themselves on account of rank and status and authority attached to that, do form a homogeneous group in terms of their uniform recruitment base and also because of the fact that there is no direct entry at Subedar level. Although the officers do not form the subject-matter of the present study, it goes without saying that the officers in general reflect the upper-middle class characteristics. The group of officers above the rank of Colonel still seems to have not forgotten the aristocratic traditions of Senior British Officers.

As it will be hereinafter sufficiently dealt with in the appropriate section that in terms of income, expenditure patterns, education, perceptions about self and others, etc., the ex-servicemen of the OR and JCO ranks strongly reflect the low-middle class characteristics and aspirations. The representation of Brahmins and Kshatriyas have fallen down considerably since 1857. Particularly after Independence, the influx of middle castes into the Army has been remarkable. The ORs and JCOs as a class in the Indian Army, thus, represent a typical example of the convergence of caste into class in the contemporary social milieu. Caste and class have become an almost synonymous and interchangeable analytical category in respect of ORs and JCOs who are placed in the middle of the traditional (caste) as well as the emerging (class) systems of stratification in the contemporary Indian context and can be an interesting subject for further studies on caste-class continuum.

Nature of the Problems of Ex-Servicemen

As already discussed, soldiers in India have always occupied an important place in society because of the indispensable functions that they have performed from the beginning of human civilisation. The concept of ex-servicemen is closely linked with the emergence of retirement and pensionary benefits in the British Indian Army. "The pension system" in the "British Indian Army" was designed to serve three important objects:

> *First*, it induced old and infirm soldiers to retire against the former practice of continuing in service till a very old age.
> *Secondly*, it attracted recruits and induced them during service to behave well.
> *Thirdly*, the pensioners, scattered all over the country, played an important political role. Their interest became identical with Government's and they could be relied upon to inculcate feelings of obedience and loyalty among the masses".[5]

It is needless to emphasise that despite changes in politico-economic contexts, the pensionary benefits are still performing all the three functions as mentioned above though its manifestly attributed reasons now also include maintaining the morale of the serving armed personnel by paying ex-servicemen well and ensuring attraction of fit and capable ones for its fresh recruitments.

If one may discount the elements of atrocious racial discrimination which the native ranks were subjected to suffer, coupled with the unfavourable terms and conditions and pay and allowances as against their British counterparts; the socio-economic status of the native ranks and their political leverage can be estimated as slightly better than the present day retired soldiers. Their comfortable situation in society after their release from the Army, however, was hardly an end-product of any conscious effort by the British Government. The natives joined the British army more for the pride and honour of their family and community than for their self-satisfaction. The birth of modern "individual" was yet to take place and a native soldier always referred back to his family, village and caste or community while in service and returned to the same soon after retirement. The near absence of urban industrial avenues of re-settlement (or what is better termed as urban industrial pull factors) the village ties may have seemed even stronger to the contemporary serving *jawans* at the verge of retirement. The reasons for their practically singular preference to go back to the villages of their origin was substantially strengthened by the capability and eagerness of the village system to decently absorb such retired officials. The country was then ruled by an alien government. If the Britishers felt that in the retired native soldiers they have planted their trusted agents in the countryside, the villagers too felt that their association with such persons may give them some respite from the harassment and exploitation by the local functionaries of the government as well as the *Zamindars* and "other respectable men" of the society. A retired soldier of the British Indian Army was welcome man in the village also because he brought money, English wine and other consumable items into the village and more especially stories of different places, people and events especially at a time when means of communication were limited and illiteracy among the masses was rampant.

The context is largely changed now. So have the problems of ex-servicemen. The village system due to over-population lacks the capacity to provide ex-servicemen any non-competitive and respectable absorption. With the inundation of mass media and greater integration of villages with the urban/industrial socio-economic system, the charm and value of an ex-serviceman are ever on the wane. His political value as a loyal agent of an alien and powerful ruler has now completely vanished. To his amazement and utter despair he finds himself a stranger in the power game of his own village. The village economic system finds itself unable to provide him any readymade absorption and demands great initiative, innovation and drive which are the requirements fairly opposite to their prolonged professional training and conditionings in the Army.

The over-population of the countryside, large-scale industrialisation and massive recruitment into the Indian Army and consequent retrenchment have almost coincided. Their preponderance itself has somewhat acted as an eroding agent undermining their value. They are no longer considered as rare species. Men who once evoked awe and reverence from the village fold are often taken casually now and sometimes even with a sense of amusement.

If the over-population of village and its inability to provide any ready economic absorption to its own emigrated member has acted as one of the strongest desisting (push) factor, the attractions (pulls) of the urban and industrial towns, too, have largely tempted them and have shaken the ex-servicemen's commitment to return to their villages. This is not to say that the urban/industrial centres have great employment avenues and their past skills and training have any direct and readymade adaptation in the civil/industrial production system. Thus, an ex-serviceman now hardly gets a red-carpet welcome in either the urban or the industrial centre. Nevertheless, the crucial point is that he now has a choice, a choice to break his ties with the place of his origin, a choice not to remain obliged and bound by the 'primordial loyalties' of the village system. The urban/industrial re-settlement has brought more miseries than fortunes to the ex-servicemen. At the first place he is no longer clear about his post-retirement vocation. He has to take a very hard decision because neither village nor urban/industrial system ensures any readymade job opportunity. He has to make a choice between hard and not so hard life of re-settling with his family either in the village or in the urban/industrial centre.

Socially too, villages have not remained a static entity. In an age when the country is having large-scale and rapid transformation from every angle – in a matter of 10-15 years, when a *jawan* normally remains away from home on duty – the entire set-up, including relationships, outlook, etc., changes. The changes which take place in villages or urban/industrial centres are not the same which take place in him in course of his training in the Army. He has a society of his own when he is in the Army and he tries his level best to adapt to his professional society throughout his career. By the time he leaves the Army to join back his native home, he finds a sea change in practically every sphere of life.

Although regular visits to one's village on leave and frequent exchanges of letters from home maintain contact with family and village society, but when it comes to stay permanently in the village, one is virtually compelled to re-socialise once again. The problems of ex-servicemen are thus a part of the general problems of uncontrollable unemployment and fast changing society in all its ramifications. They cannot afford to tackle the problems of finding a decent second career employment in isolations. This is because their ability to grab a job in the civil life depends much on their pulling the strings of social connection as the latter depends upon a decent placement in the production system. Most of them must forget the norms of an assured set-up where everything was regulated to minutest precision and everything was provided for and readily forthcoming without asking. The ex-servicemen now must always struggle in a generally precarious state of affairs until they succeed in grabbing some assured or stable position.

Although every citizen is faced with the problem of unemployment at his own level and has to confront with the stress of fast-changing society, the ex-servicemen feel it rather painfully for a variety of reasons. Some problems of everyday reality get accentuated for the ex-servicemen, for, they are used to a different world in which they did not have to struggle for their daily existence. The pampered now feel neglected. They are required to come out of their professional inertia. At the place of mute obedience to commands, great drive and initiative are wanted. The army training works as an impediment in exploiting the few opportunities available in the highly competitive world which an ex-serviceman joins. The benefits enjoyed in service makes him feel more deprived and neglected as compared to his civilian competitors for the same job or occupation.

Their problems become highly peculiar and specialised as they are made to leave a job at an age when the social responsibilities of an average ex-serviceman are at its peak. He is out of job when his children are growing and most of them are in school. His income, benefits and privileges are suddenly reduced to the bare minimum at a time when he requires them most. Lack of entrepreneurial skill and unfamiliarity with the business tricks desist him from taking any risks with the money brought home in lump sum by way of gratuity, etc., which gradually gets depleted in due course in search of a job when he has to spend his hard saved money on consumable items of everyday requirement. Seldom he gets a job more satisfying than the Army. Even if he gets a job the difficulties of professional re-socialisation are to be met which are often substantial.

It is a well known and established fact that there is no one to one relationship between aging and ability to work. It is just the peculiarity of the nature of work that the serving *jawans* are required to leave their job when they are fully fit and agile. There are numerous professions, such as teaching, law, politics, etc., in which age works as an added advantage to the role occupant. But despite all variations associated with the peculiarities of different professions, there is a general socially acknowledged scale of active and economically significant life. Therefore, 30-60 is considered to be as most active, relevant and rewarding age-group. Even in traditional Hindu life-cycle parlance, *Grihasthashrama*, the economically and socially significant period in one's life cycle has been suggested to be between 25 and 50 years in an individual's life time.

The ORs and JCOs are out of work soon after their retirement when they are expected to work and perhaps cannot do without taking up a post-retirement remunerative work. For all these, they are practically left on their own to meet the challenges of selecting and finding out a second career job. Anxiety of an ex-serviceman heightens when he has one or two growing unmarried daughters or sisters. He feels shy to attend social functions because in such functions there will be exchange of gifts and it will greatly hurt him and demoralise his wife if his offerings are smaller than what they used to be when he was in service. Thus, he is more alienated from his kin than he used to be, while in service.

Admittedly, there are variations in the nature of the problems of ex-servicemen in respect of their ranks, family responsibilities and background, age of retirement and the region they belong to. But a general trend underlying their problems is the sense of deprivation that they seem to carry when they evaluate themselves in terms of past perks and privileges or in relation to the civilians – of equal status, of like background and qualifications – enjoying their heyday of professional career. The educated and articulate ex-servicemen often summarise their sense of deprivation in the following stanza of Francis Quarles composed three centuries ago:

"God and soldier Men alike adore
When at the brink of danger, not before,
The danger past, alike are both requited,
God is forgot, and the brave soldier slighted."[6]

It is said that a soldier 'has a dangerous role in

war and thankless role in peace'.[7] The early retirement deprives ex-servicemen even from the dangerous or thankless role. The early retirement brings about loss of work, money and status which they face amidst fast increasing family responsibilities. The higher ranks seem to be much worried about their loss of *izzat*. Like the epigrams just cited above, an epitaph from the Kohima War Cemetery is also popularly quoted, emphasising the sacrifices of the soldiers:

"When you go home
Tell them of us,
For your tomorrow
We gave our today."[8]

The problems of ex-servicemen can, therefore, be summed up as inadequacy of institutionalised means in the wake of ever-increasing cultural goals. It is not just the disjunction between their cultural goals and institutionalised means. They feel somewhat punctured when privileges and facilities enjoyed while in service are abruptly withdrawn from them as if they suddenly tumbled down the cliff. They face retirement at an age when the cultural goals in terms of family responsibilities have increased and they become accustomed to a set living as a result of routine nature of their job, regular income and privileges associated with a particular rank.

At the time of joining the Indian Army a young recruit is usually a bachelor. By the time he becomes an ex-serviceman he is father of at least two growing children with his aging wife who has missed her husband's regular company throughout his Army career. In a situation when the demand from his growing kids and wife are at its peak, his post-retirement monthly income roughly gets reduced to one-third of his last pay drawn. Viewed this way, for a family of four inclusive or exclusive of the ex-serviceman, his cultural goals in terms of family responsibilities increase twelve-fold as the institutionalised means to meet such goals get reduced to one-fourth. The pension thus drawn is far too insufficient, so petty and meagre to meet the increasing responsibilities associated with cultural goals of wider amplitude. He is compelled to look for additional sources of income through whatever means. And the very process of a hunt for the second career and craving for compensating all that he has lost – economically and socio-psychologically – have been adequately treated in the introductory chapter as a process of "re-settlement".

Approaches to Resettlement

The fact that the Indian ex-servicemen face a number of problems, as outlined just above, is specially recognised by the suffering ex-servicemen and the Government. Re-settlement is conceived as an accepted method for the amelioration of their problems. Thus, when it is asked: "What is the solution to the problems of the ex-servicemen?", the invariable reply is: "Re-settlement". But before this question acquires its significance, another set of questions are already assumed to have been answered implicitly, namely: "Why the ex-servicemen be re-settled at all?" Or, "Why their problems be treated with greater sense of importance and urgency?" Answer to these questions is not just one. These involve various arguments, rationalisations, justifications and viewpoints, firstly, on part of the suffering ex-servicemen, receiving or claiming to receive re-settlement benefits and, secondly, on part of the Government always keeping extra-sensitive ear for even their feeblest voice of discontent. Thus, in the last section of the present chapter, we intend to present the viewpoints of both the ex-servicemen and Government regarding the necessity and relevance of re-settlement which we have culled from our field-work.

The rationale given by the ex-servicemen (individual respondents) in support of receiving or croaking about the existing facilities differs from person to person and from place to place. But a general trend underlying their argument points towards deprivation and subsequent compensation theory. If asked that early retirement is engrained in the nature of the job and they were aware of this condition at the time of joining the Army – they do not deny the fact. But they are apt to compare their present situation with that of the past. The comparison implicitly indicates the rising professionalisation in the industrial arena and the power and prestige enjoyed by them as well as other comparable civilian governmental functionaries. They feel to have slid down in the general power and prestige structure of society. This they call in their words as "erosion of their *izzat*" and they seem naturally to be quite concerned about that. The reasons assigned for the loss of their *izzat* in the fact that they have to beg assistance and support from the civil institutions. Whereas the milder lots from the ex-servicemen ask for more speedier and adequate treatment to their problems pertaining to the search of second career – the more vocal and aggressive ones are against the very concept of second career. They advocate that no serving *jawan* should be made to look for the second career. It should be the responsibility of the State to provide them a comparable decent job *suo motu* as soon as they are considered unfit for serving in the Army merely for the reason that they have attained a particular age which makes them unfit for the Defence Services. They say that the solution lies in "lateral placement" in civilian jobs which should become a part of the contract before joining the Army. They count innumerable forces and agencies where they can be easily absorbed and prove their utility. But this is a call for the future which pertains to the ex-servicemen of tomorrow.

The currently released armymen, though not many in number, complain that they are robbed of their youth and in the middle age they are made to lead a difficult life of penury with their family members. That they have sacrificed their youth for the defence of the country and, therefore, the middle age should be comfortable, as is the case with their civilian counterparts. Thus, it is argued that they must adequately be compensated for the strains and risks that they took while in services and for the deprivations which they feel having received after their release.

From the Government side, the need for re-settlement of ex-servicemen got due recognition with their emerging problems after the heavy release of *jawans* who were recruited on large-scale basis during Indo-China and Indo-Pak wars. The first justification given by the Government side for the quick and satisfactory re-settlement of ex-servicemen seems to be to keep up the morale of the standing Army. "Keep up the morale of the Army" appears to be the prime motivating factor on the Government side for arranging their re-settlement. The Government seems to be much concerned about the slogan '*jawans* of today are the ex-servicemen of tomorrow'. The serving armymen cannot remain oblivious to or unconcerned about the problems of their retired colleagues if the problems they have to face exceed reasonable limits. Further, the deteriorating conditions of the ex-servicemen may discourage the talented and competent young men to join the Army.

Next to the morale theory, the prevention of deviant individual/collective behaviour theory works as one of the major approaches for re-settlement among the Government circle. The reports of deviant behaviour by the ex-servicemen are not rare to find out from the newspapers. Their indulgence in robbery, dacoity, etc., have been reported from time to time. Although such incidents occurred only once in a blue moon, the very fact that they create a lasting impact on the general public mind goes to prove that there is a different standard of morality in people's mind in respect of an ex-serviceman's behaviour. It is least expected of them to indulge in daylight robbery and dacoity. The sample of the occurrences of deviant behaviour that may be considered as 'normal' for a great number of groups in society becomes 'pathological' in case of ex-servicemen. Although it is a matter of independent research to find out the reasons for such deviant behaviour from individual accused ex-serviceman, the objective fact of struggle for the search of second career and impacts of professional and social dislocations may provide some answers for their abnormal behaviour. The Government is aware that they are well trained persons equipped with arms, etc., and once they are out of control, individually or otherwise, they can create problems for the Government. A satisfied person rarely turns a deviant. Therefore, Government does not want to breed dissatisfaction among this strategic section of society and always tries to take a step ahead in resolving their problems obviating their hurdles and difficulties in order to keep them satisfied.

Apart from the individual deviant actions, what cautions the policy-makers with greater sense of urgency is their association, direct or indirect, in any violent movement. As it will be seen subsequently, by their very nature, the ex-servicemen are not likely to become a major political force and take part in political movements actively. Their open involvement in any violent movement is unlikely not only because they come from the middle class but also due to the fact that they are governed by special rules which prohibit them from taking up such an action or lines. Their overt involvement in socially disapproved movement may disqualify them from getting the pensionary and other benefits which are quite substantial by any standard if not adequate. Nevertheless, their clandestine support to any violent movement is not ruled out and their personal dissatisfaction in terms of re-settlement may be one of the many important causes. But wherever they have lent support to the violent movements, their impact has been limited geographically and local extra-economic (chiefly political) factors have weighed heavier than their dissatisfaction on account of poor re-settlement measures.

The third important approach to re-settlement is guided by the manpower management theory. It is believed that due to the inability of the Government to suitably employ their released services personnel in their employable age, there is great economic loss to the State and society. Although it is difficult to make a cost-benefit analysis of the money lost because of their deployment to some field other than the one in which they were initially trained in the Army and also the loss of the money that was invested for such training, it is commonsense understanding that their release from the Services in physically and mentally active and professionally efficient age leads to colossal waste of money. No doubt the Government is fully alive to this problem and by various notifications of its different ministries from time to time, as many as 296 service trades have been so far equated with the civil trades. This has been done with a view that the retired Army personnel do not have to waste time in justifying their worth and the doubts of employing civil institutions are also cleared about their qualifications and training in civil phraseology. The Directorate of Training of DGR has compiled a reference book entitled *Equation of Service Trades with Civil Trades* which contains Equation of Service Certificates/Examinations, Equation of Army Trades, *Equation of Army Trades* by various Agencies, Equation of Naval Trades, Equation of Air Force Trades and Equation of Common Trades in Three Services. The compilation is commendable inasmuch as it clears the doubts of various Government agencies enlightening them as to where the vacancies for ex-servicemen lie and they are interested in getting employed there.

Another strand of the conformists of manpower planning approach believes that they can play a vital role in environmental protection and large-scale tree plantation as also they can become the trusted and natural sepoys of the proposed 'national integration force' to combat any communal riot. Yet others see them as entrepreneurs full of resources, drive and initiative. The conviction is demonstrable in a separate Directorate of Self-Employment in the DGR. It remains to be seen, and we shall discuss the matter subsequently, whether such laudable expectations from the ex-servicemen have any basis or not – and whether as successful entrepreneurs they are ready to come up to the expectations of the Government and its people.

We find that there are as many approaches to re-settlement as justifications offered for it. No simple approach can be taken as the dominant one for the kinds of re-settlement benefits that are being offered now. All the approaches seem to have strengthened one another and their cumulative effect has been the general realisation of the need for speedy and adequate solution to the problems of ex-servicemen.

NOTES

1. *Report of the High Level Committee on the Problems of Ex-Servicemen*, 1984, Govrnment of India, Ministry of Defence, p.16.
2. 4.6 "An 'ex-Serviceman' means a person, who has served in any rank whether as a combatant or non-combatant in the Regular Army, Navy and Air Force of the Indian Union and,

   (i) who retired from the service after earning his/her pension, or
   (ii) who has been boarded out of the service on medical grounds attributable to military service or circumstances beyond his control and awarded medical or other disability pension, or
   (iii) who has been released from the service as a result of reduction in establishment, or
   (iv) who has been released from the service after completing the specific period of engagement, otherwise than at his own request, or by way of dismissal, or discharge on account of misconduct or inefficiency and has been given a gratuity.

   4.7 Territorial Army personnel of the following categories shall also be considered as ex-servicemen:

   (a) Pension-holders for continuous embodied service.
   (b) Disabled Territorial Army personnel with disability attributable to military service.
   (c) Gallantry award winners.

   4.8 Defence personnel, who on retirement from service would come under the category of ex-servicemen as defined in paras 4.6 and 4.7 above on retirement, will be permitted to apply for re-employment: availing themselves of all concessions one year before the completion of the specified term of engagement, where applicable. This should be subject to the clear understanding that they will be permitted to leave the uniform only after the completion of the one year period" (HLC : 1984).

The above definition has since been accepted by the Government w.e.f. 2nd July, 1987.

3. The categories excluded for the purpose of the present study are as follows:

    (i) All female persons from all the three forces of the Indian Union.
    (ii) All who have served in any rank whether as combatant or non-combatant in the Navy and Air Force of the Indian Union.
    (iii) All who have served above the rank of Subedar Major in the Regular Army of Indian Union, and
    (iv) All who have been boarded out of service on medical grounds attributable to military service or circumstances beyond their control and awarded medical or other disability pension, or
    (v) Who have been released from the service as a result of reduction in establishment, or
    (vi) Who have been released from service after completing the specific period of engagement, otherwise than at their own request, or by way of dismissal, or discharge on account of misconduct or inefficiency and have been given a gratuity, and
    (vii) All Territorial Army Personnel.

4. The concepts of settlement, re-settlement and rehabilitation have already been defined in Chapter I.
5. Saksena, K.M.L., *op. cit.*, p.213. Quoted from Note on Orgn. of Native Army of India, by H.W. Norman, dt. 11 Oct., 1875, M.D. Progs, May 1876, No.52: Encl.F.Ch.V.
6. Epigrams quoted in O.P. Sharma, *Military Law in India* (Bombay, 1973), p.2 from Chap. E.W. Buch, *Salute to the Soldier*, 1966, p.2.
7. *Ibid.*, quoted from Anthony Varrier, *An Army of the Sixties*, 1966.
8. *High Level Committee Report on Problems of Ex-Servicemen*, Government of India, (New Delhi, 1984), Quoted by Shri K.P. Singh Deo, Chairman, HLC in his foreword to the said report, p.xiii.

4

THE STUDY DESIGN AND TECHNIQUE OF DATA COLLECTION

BEFORE EMBARKING upon the present study, the researcher was closely associated with a Security Agency in Bihar which has been recruiting and placing the ex-servicemen of the region on a large scale. It is this association which provided the tentative hypothesis and rough framework for the present work, besides injecting usual passion and commitment in the subject-matter which is considered necessary for the selection of an appropriate research problem.

What was available in the form of secondary sources until August 1983 was *A Guide to Resettlement of Ex-Servicemen* of 1976 edition. A 1984 version of the same was procured subsequently by the end of that year, which gave a rough idea about the specific schemes of the Government currently being followed for the re-settlement of ex-servicemen. A monthly magazine, called *The Indian Ex-Servicemen*, is another source which is published by the All-India Ex-Services League (AIXL) since 1964. The magazine mainly focuses on the League's perceptions of the ex-servicemen's problems.

The High Level Committee Report on Problems of Ex-Servicemen

It was only in April 1984 that the Government

constituted a High Level Committee (HLC) to look into the problems of ex-servicemen and suggest ways and means for their betterment. In September 1984, this important report was submitted to the Government and was made available to the general public a few months later in printed form.

The HLC report was a valuable outline of the problems relating to ex-servicemen and it had suggested a number of methods to resolve their problems. It also had certain important statistical details.

The report, though a commendable exercise on the part of the Government in appreciation of the ex-servicemen's problems and the suggesting ways and means for their improvement, has the following limitations:

(i) Methodology adopted for getting at the root of the problem is not based on scientific principles. The committee's "appropriate questionnaires to all States and Union Territories, Ex-Servicemen Leagues and Associations as also to the individual ex-servicemen" are neither reproduced anywhere in the report nor is there any information about the number of duly filled in questionnaires received by the committee (HLC, 1984, p. 5). The report has simply reiterated the existing notions about the problems of ex-servicemen by adding up some of the points here and there on the suggestions of vested interests, such as the AIXL and other vocal elements, among the ex-servicemen.

(ii) The problems of the silent majority, i.e., those of the retired Other Ranks and Junior Commissioned Officers, have been greatly neglected.

(iii) No attempt, whatsoever, has been made to

analyse the nature of the problem. There are, of course, a few enumerations and illustrations but they are totally devoid of any analysis in depth. The problems have been put down hurriedly and haphazardly without any scientific classification. Further, there is practically no attempt to go into the reasons of a particular problem, the understanding of which might have thrown some new light on the solution of the many long-standing and pressing problems of the ex-servicemen.

(iv) The HLC report views problems through the specific programmes of the DGR and other institutions officially entrusted to "re-settle" the ex-servicemen. Accordingly, the contents of the report have also been chapterised. It would have been more appropriate to first examine the problems and then suggest specific solutions for it. Such an exercise would have also pointed out possible changes in the existing institutional arrangements entrusted with the responsibility to re-settle ex-servicemen.

(v) Due to the inadequate sensitisation to the problems of ex-servicemen, the Committee has recommended a number of measures which do not really cater to the needs of ex-servicemen.

(vi) The idea of finding an entrepreneur out of ex-servicemen is erroneous – the age, social background and prolonged professional socialisation sharply go against the basic principles of entrepreneurship.

Despite the above-mentioned limitations, the researcher, all the same found the Report of the Committee a great help to formulate his study design and hypotheses in the light of valuable statistical details and statements of facts contained in it.

Other Source Materials Consulted[1]

Apart from various issues of the *Indian Ex-Servicemen, A Guide to Resettlement of Ex-Servicemen* (1984) and *Report of the High Level Committee on Problems of Ex-Servicemen* (1984), the researcher was benefited by the following booklets/magazines:

Books

1. *Kya aur kaise? Bhutpurva O.R. evam J.C.O., KO Punarvas Mein Sahayata*, 1982, DGR, G.O.I. (In Hindi)
2. *Ex-Serviceman as entrepreneur*, 1982, DGR, G.O.I.
3. *A Handbook of Resettlement Training of Ex-Servicemen*, 1984, DGR, G.O.I.
4. *A Handbook of Self-Employment of Ex-Servicemen*, 1984, DGR, G.O.I.
5. *Preparing Ex-Servicemen for Self-Employment*, 1986, DGR, G.O.I.
6. *Memorandum and the Articles of Association of the Indian Ex-Services Leagues*, 1986, AIXL, New Delhi.
7. *SEMFEX SCHEME* (Self-Employment for Ex-Servicemen), 1987, DGR, G.O.I.
8. *Equation of Service Trades with Civil Trades*, (Undated), DGR, G.O.I.

Magazines

1. *Indian Ex-Servicemen* (Monthly Publication of the Indian Ex-Services League), New Delhi, Vols. I-XXV.
2. *Sainik Punarvas*, DGR, G.O.I., New Delhi, vols. I-II.

The Time Frame

The study is limited to the period between 1981-85. This means that only those ex-servicemen who retired between 1981-85 were interviewed in the study. Re-settlement, as we have defined earlier, is a typical synchronic problem and, therefore, a problem of high sociological importance. No doubt, all retired and living personnel of the Indian Defence Forces are ex-servicemen and all may have problems of some kind or other. But the problem of "re-settlement" is limited only to the currently retired ex-servicemen. It is only the currently retired ex-servicemen who face the shock and trauma of re-settlement which might, of course, tend to diminish with the passage of time. Five years time was also considered a sufficient period for an individual ex-serviceman to find his socio-psychological and economic re-settlement in civilian life.

Another reason for limiting the period was the employability of the of the ex-servicemen. A great number of organisations prefer to recruit the ex-servicemen within two years of their retirement.

In addition, with the passage of time, the ex-servicemen retired long before may have found their way out in the civilian life and by now their children grown up and got settled. The central focus of the study is on the re-settlement of ex-servicemen in terms of their problems relating to the search of second career and issues associated with it. The time frame thus chosen was thought to be appropriate.

The Universe

Bihar and Haryana form the spatial universe of the present study. One of the major hypothesis is that the re-settlement of ex-servicemen is better and quicker in developed regions than the under-developed ones. Keeping this in view, Bihar, an under-developed region, and Haryana, as a typical developed region were chosen for the purpose of the study. The connotations of development and under-development vary contextually. Haryana peasantry has a continuous history of participation in the Indian Army since the early period of British rule. Although the peasantry of Bihar also participated in the British Army, though for different reasons, their recruitment was deliberately discouraged after the Revolt of 1857. It is only after Independence that the recruitment to military from Bihar got adequately restored. Therefore, continuous military tradition of a region along with a history of around 200 years is examined with a region with discontinuous but chequered military tradition. This was considered a fact of high sociological importance which facilitates or hinders re-settlement.

Another marked difference between the two regions is in terms of State action for the re-settlement of ex-Servicemen by way of reservation in State Government Departments, Undertakings, etc. It will be seen that whereas Haryana tops in terms of providing reservation of seats to the ex-servicemen in Government services and other concessions, Bihar has no reservation whatsoever for its ex-servicemen. Concessions and benefits provided by Bihar Government are also superficial. The choice of the two States, therefore, has also facilitated the understanding on the impact of State patronage to ex-servicemen on their re-settlement.

In a democratic set-up, numerical predominance of a group at least partly determines its place and approachability in the Government. Haryana has a very high percentage of ex-servicemen. It is said that one out of every five belongs to a "*fauzi*" family in

Haryana. Their numerical predominance has reflected itself in the kind of concessions and benefits they received from the Haryana Government. Seldom is there any Ministry in which one or two ex-servicemen are not included to satisfy this constituency. On the contrary, in Bihar they form a negligible minority in terms of the total population of the State and hence are unable to exert as a pressure group on the Government. The importance of the size and proportion of ex-servicemen population in a given State can be understood and analysed through a comparison of Bihar and Haryana.

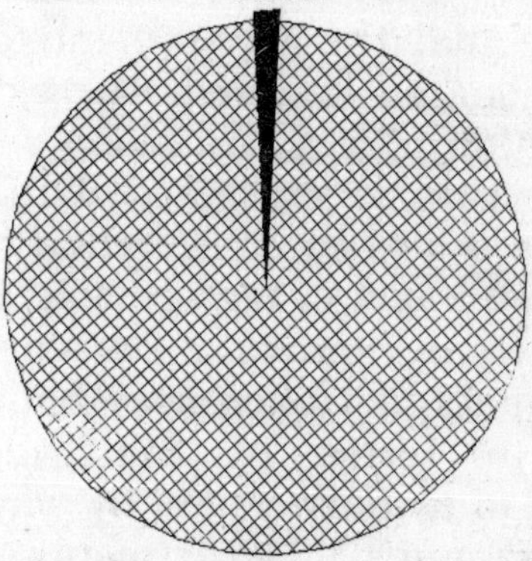

FIG. 4.1(a): Population of Ex-servicemen in Bihar (Percentage)

Bihar and Haryana, the two States selected for the present study, had the total population of 2.22 lakh and 2.18 lakh of ex-servicemen, respectively, which contributed to 1.6 per cent and 8.5 per cent of their State's population, respectively, in the year 1981.[2] The HLC has considered the necessity of reliable data regarding the population of ex-servicemen in the country. It has been recommended that the ex-servicemen be considered as a separate category in 1991 Census for the purpose of their enumeration. The percentage frequency of the population of ex-servicemen in

Bihar in Figs. 4.1(a) and 4.1(b) respectively.

FIG. 4.1(b): Population of Ex-servicemen in Haryana (Percentage)

Two districts each were selected from Bihar and Haryana for the present study. Patna and Ranchi districts have been selected from Bihar and Gurgaon and Sonepat district from Haryana. The rationale for the choice of the districts was the assumption that the ex-servicemen living in the vicinity of bigger cities have better employment opportunities than those living near smaller cities. Gurgaon and Sonepat are situated near Delhi, a very big city. Patna and Ranchi are relatively smaller cities.

The selection of districts could have been done on the basis of the size of ex-servicemen population also but in absence of any reliable data regarding their population, especially of the period selected for the purpose of the present study, made such exercise meaningless. Once it was decided that the study must explore the impact of metropolitan city of Delhi on the employment opportunity of ex-servicemen, selection of very small towns from Bihar would have been no match to Delhi for the propose of comparison. Therefore, Patna and Ranchi were selected as districts to be studied in Bihar.

While defining the ex-serviceman for the purpose

of the present study we have sufficiently deliberated upon the reasons for excluding the commissioned officers of the Indian Army as well as both men and officers coming from the Indian Air Force and the Indian Navy. To recapitulate, it may be recalled here that our universe comprises of the ex-servicemen of the Indian Army from sepoy to Subedar Major rank retired between 1981 and 1985 and stationed at districts of Patna and Ranchi in Bihar and Gurgaon and Sonepat in Haryana. The field-work was conducted between October 1985 and May 1986, i.e., in eight-month time.

The Sample

Apart from the all-India statistics of ex-servicemen referred to earlier, no district level systematic data could be procured from the respective Zila Sainik Board (henceforth referred to as ZSB) or Kendriya Sainik Board (hence forth referred to as KSB). The data reflecting the registration of ex-servicemen with ZSB, Patna and Ranchi could, however, be procured from the Rajya Sainik Board (RSB), Ptana, for the period 1984-1987. The difficulty with these data is that they represent the ex-servicemen of two or more districts on the basis of jurisdiction of respective ZSBs. Therefore, the figures of district Patna also include ex-servicemen of newly created Nalanda district and figures of Ranchi include Palamau, Lohardagga and Gumla districts. Thus conceived, therefore, the ex-servicemen who got registered with ZSB, Patna, in the year 1984, 1985, 1986 and 1987 are 162, 181, 248 and 361, respectively. The corresponding figure of Ranchi are 316, 255, 553, and 489. Considering the fluctuations in the annual return of the ex-servicemen in the districts and non-availability of precise and complete data, statistical interpretation and analysis of the secondary data were ruled out in the very beginning. The task now was how to elicit the needed information and create data.

In the absence of complete and reliable district-wise data, sampling had to be done rather intuitively, depending upon the time and resource available. However, before proceeding to the field, it was resolved to interview 50 ex-servicemen from each district and, as far as it was practicable, cover 10 ex-servicemen retired each year during the period 1981-85. A control card was maintained by the researcher so that the ex-servicemen retired during the period were interviewed proportionately. District-wise distribution of ex-servicemen interviewed yearwise is given in Fig. 4.2.

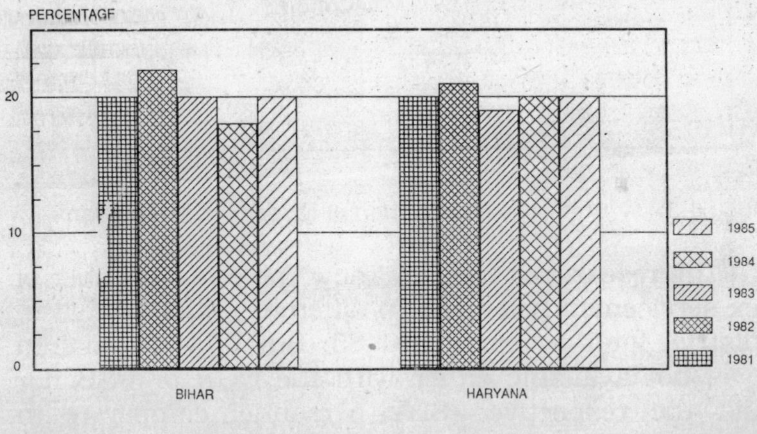

FIG. 4.2: Statewise Distribution of Ex-servicemen by Year of Retirement

It can be seen, therefore, that a fairly even distribution of ex-servicemen for the each year was maintained in each district of the two States.

Akin to the year-wise control-card, rank-wise control card was also maintained for each district in order to keep balance of the ex-servicemen in terms of rank. Army has pyramidic structure, therefore, the possibility of finding lower ranks on random visits to Pension/Treasury officers are greater than those of the higher ranks. Thus, the rank-wise control card served the purpose of maintaining a proportionate balance between JCO and Other Ranks. Statewise distribution of ex-servicemen interviewed by rank is given in Fig. 4.3.

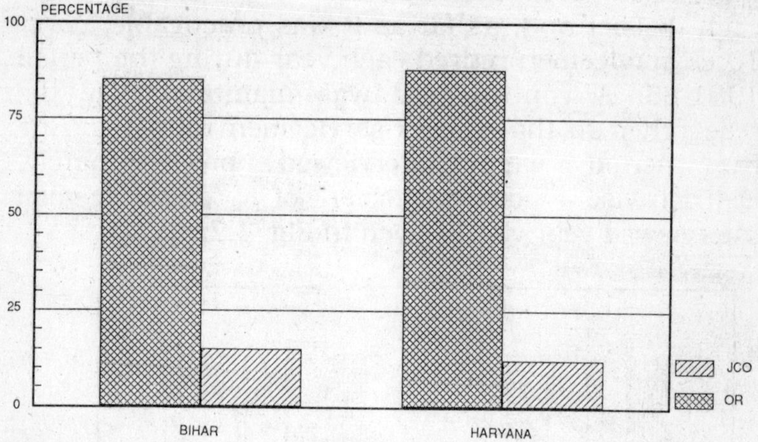

FIG. 4.3: Statewise Distribution of Ex-servicemen by Rank

The researcher tried to know the exact number of ex-servicemen belonging to different ranks in a given district for the years 1981-85. But this information was not available either with the DGR or RSB nor did the respective ZSB's personnel co-operate in providing the figure. Then the researcher tried to ascertain the normally maintained ratio of one rank as against another in the Indian Army, but even this was not made available in any definitive terms.

Officers of Subedar ranks were only a few in all the four districts where the study was conducted. In a number of cases, the researcher had to gather their names and addresses from different sources and had to visit their residence or place of work for interview. Even though there was no precise basis on which the ex-servicemen of different ranks could be stratified conclusively, Fig. 4.3 shows marked preponderance of Other Marks as compared to Junior Commissioned Officers.

Major Hypotheses

The hypotheses of the present research work have been formulated out of the classification in which we have tried to conceptually place the ex-servicemen as a significant social category. The ex-servicemen, therefore, are being viewed in the following manner for the purpose of working out a study on the patterns and problems relating to their re-settlement. Each classification, thus has given birth to one major hypothesis to be tested in the present work.

Army being a highly stratified and structured organisation, each rank is endowed with well defined status, rights and duties, and perks and privileges. The occupants of each rank have a defined retirement age, pensions and gratuity rates, etc., associated with it. Therefore, it is quite natural to expect commonality of problems relating to the ex-servicemen of each rank throughout the country as all armymen are governed by the same service conditions of the Indian Army. Since the higher the rank at which one retires, the better the post retirement pensions and perks, and the longer the age of retirement, the first hypothesis being formulated is as follows:

Higher the Rank of Retirement Better the Prospects of Resettlement

Any process require time for its completion and resettlement is no exception to this rule. Five years time has been assumed as the maximum time period in which one should feel "re-settled" or compromise with the type of living he has been able to provide for himself during that period. In other words, urge for a professional or occupational change after five years of one's retirement was considered as a remote possibility. Consequently, for the purpose of this analysis, ex-servicemen, retired in each year during the period 1981-85, have been considered as a distinct class irrespective of their rank or place of retirement. Hypothesis which is to be tested, therefore, is this:

Longer the Period from the Date of Retirement, Better the Re-settlement

The traditional Indian society was stratified on the principles of *varna* and caste. Higher position in caste hierarchy to some extent also means approachability to better social connections and material conditions. And, this persists particularly in rural India. An ex-serviceman, returning to his village, not only returns to his family but also to a caste to which the family belongs. For an ex-serviceman, therefore, the position of his caste *vis-a-vis* others determines how soon and how well he will be re-settled in his society. Therefore, hypothesis emerging out of the classification based on caste can be formulated like this:

Higher the Caste, Better the Prospects of Re-settlement

For a variety of reasons India does not have a uniform regional development. Regional inequality in terms of development has long historical roots. But in effect it means better living conditions and job-opportunity to those living in developed areas than the ones living in the under-developed ones. Thus, the developed regions have better infrastructure for the absorption of ex-servicemen returning to these areas than the under-developed ones. The very purpose of selecting two regions – one developed and the other under-developed – was to see the impact of regional development on the resettlement of ex-servicemen. Thus, the fourth hypothesis which emerges out of classification based on the State of domicile is:

The ex-servicemen are better settled in developed regions (e.g. Haryana) than in under-developed regions (e.g. Bihar)

In tune with the above-mentioned classification and the four major hypotheses, there were a large number of minor hypotheses which were formed on the basis of the instrument which was gradually developed for the purpose of final round of field-work on which the findings of the present work are based.

Techniques of Research

In the beginning of 1984, a cyclostyle questionnaire in Hindi was circulated among the ex-servicemen for pretesting in the four districts of Patna, Ranchi, Gurgaon and Sonepat. Around 40 questionnaires were thus filled in each containing 34 questions. By then, it was known that the best method of approaching ex-servicemen was to catch them at District Treasury/Pension Offices on the dates specified for the disbursal of pensions. The researcher had also come to know the functions of institutions, such as Zila Sainik Board, Rajya Sainik Board, Directorate of Re-settlement, Ex-Services League and other similar organisations. Contacts with the functionaries of these organisations and also with the knowledgeable ex-servicemen of different ranks settled in the respective districts gradually developed.

The pre-testing Interview Schedule of early 1984 was to be thoroughly revised in the beginning of 1985 for the following reasons:

(1) The questionnaires used for pre-testing were filled in by the ex-servicemen themselves. But it was found that most of them could not fill in the questionnaire without the help of the researcher. Therefore, it was decided to proceed with an interview schedule instead of a questionnaire.

(2) All the open-ended questions included in the pre-testing questionnaire were to be dropped and if necessary were to be substituted by limited choice questions.

(3) For the purpose of clarity and quantification, it was now possible to have closed questions with limited choices in the range of two to nine options against each question. One of such options was to be ticked by the researcher himself after orally obtaining and assessing the correct choice of the respondents.

(4) In light of the responses gathered from the pre-testing as well as on the basis of the findings of the HLC report, quite a number of questions of the first (pre-testing) questionnaire were considered redundant and many more were considered necessary to be added in the interview schedule.

Methods of Eliciting Information

It usually took 45-60 minutes to fill in an interview schedule form excluding the time spent on reaching the respondents and also excluding the time taken in rapport making. Since the researcher met the ex-servicemen in group, rapport making with all the respondents individually was not necessary. Once rapport was established with one of the ex-servicemen waiting to get pension in front of Treasury/Pension Office, on any pension day, rest of the work was easy. Normally, it is the first respondent who became the contact man for the day and introduced the researcher with others. Interview with the first respondent also generated interest among the surrounding ex-servicemen waiting for Payment. On any interview day, the researcher could interview roughly between four to eight ex-servicemen. The ex-servicemen of the higher ranks responded faster to the questions put than those of the lower ranks. Similarly, difficulties in explaining the questions to the lower ranks naturally were more pronounced and questions had often to be repeated or put in different words in order to obtain information.

The encounter with the first ex-Serviceman on any of the interview day was quite difficult. In order to prepare the first respondent the researcher almost invariably began with explaining to him the purpose of the work. In Bihar, especially in Ranchi district, it was pretty difficult to get co-operation from the respondents. The first reaction was hesitation, coupled with suspicion. In both the districts of Haryana, i.e., Gurgaon and Sonepat, ex-servicemen were quite co-operative and invariably they took great interest in the interview making it relatively easier. Usually the tea-stalls/*dhabas* near the Treasury/Pension Office became the place of interview. Interestingly, in Bihar it was the respondent who normally paid for the tea/ refreshment, etc., but in Haryana it was just the reverse. In Haryana, the researcher seldom sat with just one respondent, the second and the third were always ready in queue to be interviewed and they shared the bills of tea/cigarettes/refreshments, etc., on collective basis. In Haryana, again, at least on three to four occasions, the researcher was almost "*gheraoed*" by the ex-servicemen who showered on him a number of grievances and unfulfilled promises of the Government. On hearing the real purpose of research the respondents invariably asked how the exercise by the researcher was going to improve their lot and mitigate their immediate complaints. It was hard and often embarrassing to reply to such questions but the every occasion of embarrassment strengthened the researchers conviction to make an honest and incisive study of their problems. While the researcher here was impressed and sometimes embarrassed by the active participation of ex-servicemen in his fieldwork, on the contrary he was often moved by the ignorance, silence and wretched lot of his respondents particularly in Bihar. They had much poorer conditions of living and much greater problems than their *Haryanvi* counterparts. And, yet they were not as vociferous and complaining as were the ex-servicemen in Haryana.

At Treasury/Pension Offices majority of the persons waiting for pension belonged to the pre-1981 group. The ex-servicemen retired between 1981 and 1985 were a few on any day of the researcher's visit to the Pension/Treasury Office looking for his respondents. Therefore, the first sorting was done by the initial glance at the waiting pensioners. The elderly persons were just avoided and avid overtures were shown to the younger ones. Thereafter two questions were asked to ascertain whether the respondent comes within the purview of the present study. These were:

1. When did you retire?
2. Have you served the Indian Army?

If the answer to question one was, "between 1981 and 1985" that of question number two was in the affirmative, then it was settled that the person so answering should be invited for an interview.

Apart from eliciting information through interview schedule with an eye to arrive at some quantitative data, qualitative data were never ignored. The respondents who showed more interest in the subject-matter and were ready to inform more than what was being sought in the interview schedule were always encouraged. A number of respondents invited the researcher to their respective homes (in village) in each of the four districts covered for the purpose of fieldwork. It was one of the strategies of the fieldwork to visit at least one ex-serviceman of each rank in every district and observe him at home as well as at work at least for a day or two. While invitation from the ex-servicemen of Haryana was usual and natural, in the case of Bihar the researcher had to take initiative. Majority of respondents from Bihar also asked reasons for the researchers visit to their houses and places of work.

The qualitative data also got enriched by indepth interview with some knowledgeable persons and senior Army officials of the area where the fieldwork was conducted. The Director-General of Resettlement and a number of officials of the DGR gave valuable information and literature to the researcher from time to time. Similarly, Brig. Ram Singh and others of the All-India Ex-Services League and Brig. B.N. Upadhyay of Bihar unit of the AIXL apprised him of the problems of ex-servicemen at the national and the regional levels.

The researcher also participated in the rallies and *dharnas* organised by the AIXL and parallel organisations from time to time during the course of his fieldwork. The researcher used camera and a taperecorder during appropriate occasions in the course of his fieldwork. The researcher's reflections on the rallies and meetings of ex-servicemen and their political efficacy will be dealt with in the subsequent chapters.

NOTES

1. In the XI World Sociological Congress, New Delhi, 1986, the researcher met Dr. (Mrs.) M.K. Singh, Reader, Department of Sociology, Poona University. Subsequently, at Nehru Museum Library, New Delhi, he studied her book entitled *Resettlement Problems of Retired Army Officers*, New Delhi, 1985. This is a study of 140 retired army officers ranging from Captain to Brigadier of Poona and the areas surrounding it. This is a discrete study on identical problem from every angle of research. For the benefit of those pursuing serious research on "the resettlement of ex-servicemen in India" the contents of her work, however, are being produced below:

   1. Introduction, 2. The Indian Army — A Historical Perspective, 3. The Army Professionals, 4. Retirement — A Social Institution and its Problems, a Theoretical Perspective, 5. Methodology, 6. The Problems and Their Magnitude, 7. Career after Retirement, 8. Section 1: Problems in the Professional Field, Section 2: Problems in the Social Field, 9. Existing Agencies at Work and Views of the Respondents, 10. Suggestive Measures.

2. The data were taken down at DGR Office, New Delhi, which is based on the statements sent to the DGR Office by respective Rajya Sainik Boards.

5

NATURE OF RE-SETTLEMENT: Process and Patterns

TWO IMPORTANT decisions – implicit or explicit – precede before an ex-serviceman actually accepts his post-retirement life. The first is about the place where he wants to settle down and second, the type of career which he might prefer to take up. A decision regarding the two problems is determined by a number of choices available in society at a given point of time which operate as socially (external) limiting factors. The preference or suitability of one job career against the other is guided by the personal capability, ambition and limitations, which operate as personal limiting factors for an individual ex-serviceman. The two limiting factors therefore, set the ultimate boundary for an ex-serviceman, within which his decision about place and work of his post-retirement life is to be taken.

The primary focus of the present chapter is the classification and outline of those compulsions which move an ex-serviceman towards one social choice or the other regarding post-retirement life and career.

The Choice of Place

While getting released/retired the first question which arises is "where to settle down, where to go to spend the remaining part of life?" For most of the ex-servicemen, however, the answer to this question is already given, right from the day he entered into the profession of arms and more so from the date he got married.

Although one may find it surprising, the process of resettlement for an individual begins from the day he joins Army. His decision regarding the choice of place of resettlement is taken well before he is retired/released from the Army. Usually, for a *jawan*, the date of entry into the Army and the date of marriage have a close proximation. These coincidences tend to strengthen the jointness of family, even though it is generally being held that joint families in India are ebbing away and there has been a sea change even in the existing 'jointness' in the families as compared to the past.

It is evident from Fig. 5.1 that most of the ex-servicemen families (49% from Bihar and 64% from Haryana) live in the 'joint family'.

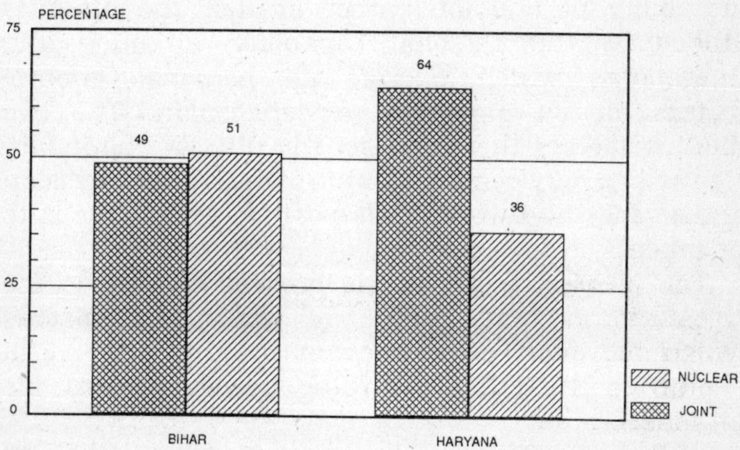

FIG. 5.1: Statewise Distribution of Ex-servicemen by Type of Family

The professional requirement is such that usually the spouse (and kids, if any) of a serving *jawan* has to be kept away from the place of his duty. In the early phase of the career, it is difficult to find a family station. In most of the cases wherever the decision in respect of choice of residence for the spouse and kids are to be taken, the spontaneous and often implied response is 'with his parents' and in the paternal house. In case the father is not alive, the preferential residence is with the brother, usually the elder one.

A serving *jawan*'s wife and children either staying with the father or (if not alive) with the brother(s) enjoy his co-parcenary rights in the family. The relationship between the family of the serving *jawan* and his paternal relatives reflects the tendency of strengthening the joint family system. The mere fact of a *jawan* existing in a family gives an indication that family of orientation, even if nuclear, will become joint soon after he gets married, for his wife is to be left with this parents when he goes out for duties after spending brief annual vacations of about two months, every year.

When a young boy joins army he is in his teens. Much depends upon his parents whether he should join the Army or not or even if he should think of it or not. Since the father of a serving *jawan* is in picture right from the day his son joins the Army and he is active partner in his decision-making process, the responsibility of taking care of his son's would-be-wife and kids is implied right from the day he sent him to the Army. That is why *'Inami jagir'* is given to the parents of the only son being inducted into the Army, or only two sons, or three or more sons. Parents get such facilities also in recognition of the fact that they are taking extra responsibility of keeping and taking care of the family of his son(s) apart from the general incentive given for motivating his son(s) to join Army.

There are many factors which (contribute to the

jointness of the family and) ensure the return of ex-serviceman into his joint family soon after retirement/release. First of all he visits the joint family regularly throughout his professional career for the satisfaction of some of his basic psychological needs. In the earlier years of marriage, it is the gratification of sexual desire which is paramount and often draws him towards his spouse who normally resides with her in-laws. Later on, when his children grow, need for providing them affection and security start weighing equally heavy. When the kids grow up, in case of daughters, it is the anxiety about their marriage which is more important than education and career which is more applicable in case of sons. For providing and managing all these, he has constantly to depend upon his relatives. It is a seldom that a currently retired JCO or Other Rank is also the *Karta* of the joint family. Normally *Karta* is the father, if alive. Otherwise the *Karta* may be the uncle or the elder brother of the self (Fig. 5.2).

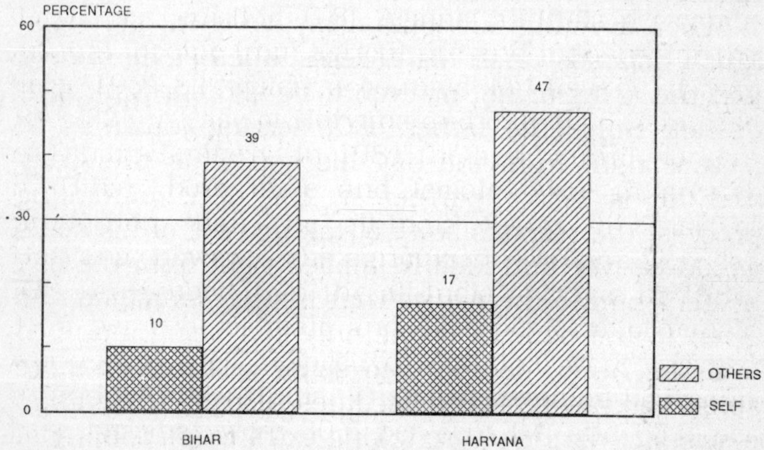

FIG. 5.2: *Karta*, if Ex-Serviceman Living in a Joint Family

So long the serving son is in the field duty, he invariably requires the help of his parents or brothers. Only in rare cases the help of father-in-law and brother-in-law as against his own father or brothers is required. But it is not only the son who requires the help of his parents/brothers, etc., so that his wife and children are taken care of but also all those who claim to have done their duty towards his wife and children look upon him for certain favour or help. The very first benefit, though non-material, which they receive is the 'goodwill' aspect. Performing the 'social functions' of husband in absence of a *jawan* on duty, the *karta* of the joint family thereby acquires goodwill among his friends and relatives which is of immense social value and significance. Goodwill in every case has a tendency to make the person powerful from where it comes – whether from the economic, social or political quarters. Then in a great many cases, the serving son or brother is the only government functionary which adds to their prestige and power in the social system to which the *karta* belongs. Further, an armyman is a regular source of income. His regular remittances in lieu of the monthly provisions arranged for his wife and kids are invariably the only regular cash flowing to the members of the joint family. His wife is an additional hand in the service of all in the joint family. Often, he brings subsidised items, such as blankets, watches, rum, etc., to his family members (of orientation). He is asked to contribute some cash for his sister's marriage or for niece's marriage, or for some other important social functions or for family problems such as meeting the requirements of seeds, irrigation, electricity or some developmental plan of the joint family in which capital investment is required. He is also required to be present during the harvest seasons all through his service career and often he manages leave during those periods and his services are fully utilised for that purpose, too. In certain cases he is also asked to avenge the grudge and gravel of his family members which they have piled up for him over the year. A serving *jawan*, therefore, remains useful everywhere. The State, the society and the family, all equally benefit from him. His family members and relatives, therefore, need him as much as he needs their help and attention.

Towards the close of his career, however, the need for having closer ties with his family members get invariably accentuated especially when he has a growing daughter to get married for which he will at least require the liaisoning functions to be performed by his brothers and relatives. Similarly, the old parents and brothers/relatives of the retiring officer, too, show all overtures of red-carpet welcome because they know well what money and benefit he will carry home. The glamour and prospects of getting a share out of the benefits arriving is ever alluring. Thus, much before retirement the choice for the place of re-settlement where he should look for a second career is almost clear in majority of cases.

Apart from the push and pull factors which are generated by the joint family ties in favour of his re-settlement in the area of his ancestral joint dwelling, the considerations for reviving the contacts of his old peer group, with the caste/community members and the secondary and tertiary relatives are also important. He does expect some sympathy, favour from his already existing civilian contacts and thinks it wise to cultivate the same rather than taking a major social risk by choosing an alien environment for re-settlement. Additionally, the Army socialsation also promotes close ties to one's sub-cultural group. The regimental living tends to promote the local social network.

Not only that, the society other than the place where he grew up before getting recruited to the Army is socially alien for him and in a great many places in the contemporary Indian local situations, he may even feel scared to settle down. Apart from the requirements to adjust with ever-changing, unpredictable and deteriorating local political situation, the barriers of language and culture also weigh equally heavy in discouraging him from considering any offer (which is virtually none) from outside one's linguistic and cultural zone. There are all possibilities of seeking social security from relatives and community members as a matter of right with full confidence. The elements of social security are almost nil even if the situation of the alien local setting is not hostile. It is almost impossible to escape labelling by insiders which, on a great many occasions, exceeds its socialising humour and warm contents rendering the outsider into social and psychological defensive position. There are certain occasions on which even after returning to his own village, he is treated as an outsider, but such cases are few and far between and wherever they occur the *fauzi* has full moral courage and right to counter or brush aside their sneer and offending enthusiasm towards him.

For an individual retired/released Army JCO or *jawan*, the factors relating to the choice of place of re-settlement can, therefore, be summed up in a formula like this:

$$CPR = DEcp \times Icp - Acpp,$$

where

CPR signifies "Choice of place for Resettlement",
DEcp signifies "Duration of Estrangement from Cultural Pull"
Icp signifies "Intensity of Cultural Pull of the native place"
Acpp signifies "Alien Cultural Push".

Where the cultural pull of native place is zero or in the negative, the retired/released officer may think of finally settling down anywhere in India, but such situation is rare to find. But if it does happen the ex-serviceman will prefer the areas where alien push is zero i.e., cosmopolitan urban or industrial setting. The situation of the ex-servicemen may be contrasted with the politically distressed group, such as refugees, war victims, etc., or economically and socially distressed individuals prepared to pick up anything from anywhere for sheer survival. The ex-servicemen, on the contrary, are those having firm social base in the place of their origin. In addition, they have regular income by way of pension and assured concessions and sympathy of the Government. The pension amount and assured benefits and concessions in terms of medical, canteen, housing facilities, etc., provide material conditions for them to wait and try for a second career job in the vicinity of native place where they have returned.

The Choice of Work

Quest for the second career begins once an ex-serviceman returns to the place of his choice after discharge or release. The choice of place, therefore, conditions the choice of work of a person. In other words, the opportunities available in the local employment market puts the outer boundary for an ex-serviceman from which he can exercise his option for preferring one job opportunity to another. The supply situation or the number of skilled persons available for the job that an ex-serviceman is trying to get makes the task of job-seeking either easier or tougher for him. Therefore, in view of the varying different demand-supply situations in the labour market from region to region and State to

State and also the different wage structures provide enough substance to the assumption that the sheer fact of differences in the social-economic and political conditions of any two regions would make the process of re-settlement of an ex-serviceman either simpler or tougher. Regional factors contributing to the re-settlement of ex-serviceman, such as, cultural tradition, economic development and political support, etc., have been dealt with separately. Here we will concentrate on some general factors which determine the choice of work of ex-servicemen.

Through our preliminary enquiries it was gathered that a number of ex-servicemen seeking employment do not sit idle. They actively participate in the family farming while looking for another suitable job. It would have been erroneous to put them either in unemployed or self-employed category. A new category named "self-employed seeking job" was, therefore, included in the final instrument as it is evident from Fig. 5.3.

Majority (48%), therefore, are employed, followed by self-employed seeking job (23.5%), self-employed not wanting job (14.5%) and unemployed (14%). As it will be clear in the next Chapter, the unemployed ex-servicemen are the ones who do not have any prospects for getting self-employment for a variety of reasons. Thus, 85.5 per cent of the ex-servicemen show their preferences for re-employment and only 14.5 per cent have preferred self-employment as their post-retirement career.

It should be made clear at the very outset that the thinking process regarding choice of work begins much before the date of retirement. Usually, those dreaming of some self-employment are more clear about their future re-settlement than those who thought they would get some or other employment. However, those consciously opting for self-employment venture are few. There is direct correlation between premeditated clarity of goal in favour of self-employment and success. Those taking up self-employment as residual option have invariably failed. These points have been explained in greater detail with the help of field data in the next chapter.

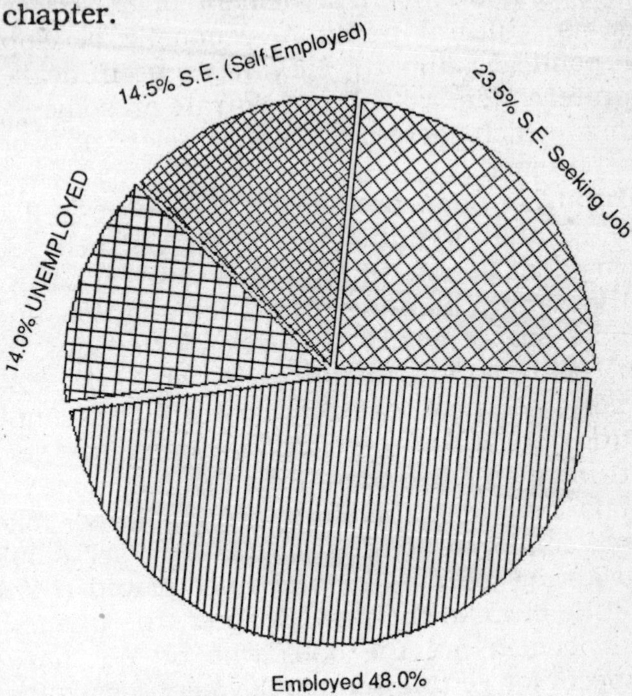

FIG. 5.3: Occupatitonal Status of Ex-servicemen (Bihar and Haryana)

In the present section we intend to examine the issues involved in the processes relating to the choice of re-employment or self-employment as post-retirement career of the ex-servicemen.

Re-employment

Special facilities in terms of reservation and relaxation in age and qualification are given to ex-servicemen so as to ensure that they are re-employed quickly without much difficulty. The rationale for making special arrangement for the placement of ex-servicemen in their post-retirement career can be explained in terms of personal and social necessity. The rationale of personal necessity is subsumed in the very fact that most of them (the ORs) get retired between 32-41 years of age. Their early retirement as the requirement of the job is, therefore, inevitable. If youthful profile of the Army is to be maintained they must leave the Army before they get old. Thus, they get retired while still in the age-group which is socially very crucial. They are married and often have school going kids. With growing family responsibilities, many of them do not have fixed assets, such as land, family business, etc., to fall back upon. Thus, for quite a few of them, the only source of running the family, educating the children and meeting expenses according to the status attained just before retirement/release, is their re-employment.

The rationale of social necessity is best summed up in the words of HLC as:

> "While in the service, many of them would have received specialised training. It would, therefore, be in the national interest that this reservoir of trained and disciplined manpower is gainfully and effectively utilised in different walks of life" (HLC, 1984, p.19).

The crux of the matter is that investments incurred in the specialised training of ex-servicemen, while in service, should not be allowed to go waste or unultilised. It takes time and money to impart to an individual certain specialised skill. Similarly, it also requires some time and money to make a man culturally rich to enable him to understand the importance of hard work, discipline, sincerity to work and honesty in ones dealings, etc. Therefore, the training acquired in the Army, both technical and moral, should not be allowed to go waste. For the purpose of avoiding duplication in training for getting a civilian post and thereby saving immense time and money, "the DGR has equated a total of 211 military trades with current civilian trades as laid down by the DGET" (HLC: 1984, p. 48). The equation of military trades and qualifications, if accepted by all the State Governments for the purpose of re-employment of ex-servicemen will not only avoid duplication in training but will also ensure that an ex-serviceman usually gets the occupational status of the kind which he occupied before his retirement/release.

Every year, roughly about 16,000 ex-servicemen are being helped in getting re-employment (*Military Year Book*, 1986: p. 83). In other words, one out of every four retiring servicemen can think of getting a job with the help of the facilities and concessions extended by the Government. Preparation for seeking civilian re-employment begins 15 months before the retirement of a serving officer who is supposed to submit four copies of duly filled in application form for registration in the concerned ZSB. Even if he fails to submit the form through proper channel while in service, he can get himself registered at concerned ZSB after showing his Discharge Certificate.

> "The Government of India has granted reservations for employment of ex-servicemen in civil posts as under :
>
> (a) Ten per cent of the vacancies in Group 'C' posts and 20 per cent in group 'D' posts.
> (b) 14-1/2 per cent and 24-1/2 per cent in groups

'C' and 'D' posts, respectively, in public sector undertakings and Banks.

(c) As far as Groups 'A' and 'B' posts are concerned there is reservation of 10 per cent in the posts of Assistant Commandants in the Parliamentary Forces only" (HCL, p.20).

The State Governments have reserved their posts of different types in varying percentages for the purpose of civil employment of ex-servicemen.[1] The States providing maximum reservation, however, are Himachal Pradesh, Haryana and Punjab and, on the other hand the States which do not provide any reservation facilities at all are Bihar, Kerala, Maghalaya and Nagaland.

Since the opportunities available are limited and vary from State to State, the choice of employment is determined by the interplay of existing opportunities where the work is being sought for and the ex-servicemen's ability to avail of the opportunity in his favour as against other ex-servicemen competing for the same post.

Question 14 of the *Employment Index Card* of the Directorate General of Resettlement (DGR) puts the question as follows :

"Whether willing to serve:

(a) Anywhere in India ? Yes/No.
(b) In Home State only? Yes/No.
(c) In paramilitary forces? Yes/No.
(d) In foreign countries? Yes/No."

Our enquiries reveal that most of the applicants have shown their willingness to serve in their home States only, a fact which was also correlated by the DGR office, though precise data were not made available.

Figure 5.4, however, clearly shows that the ex-servicemen prefer to work nearer home. But preference to serve in one's own State tells only the half story about the choice of place where the work (job) is intended.

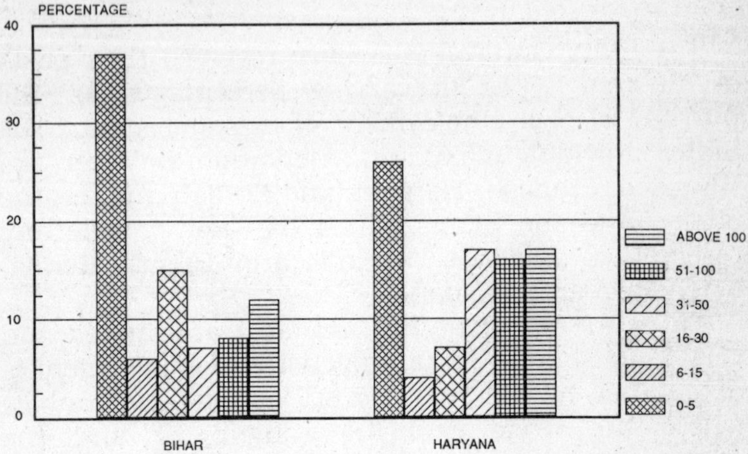

FIG. 5.4: **Distance Between Home and Work-Place (in km)**

The truth is that an ex-servicemen wants employment as close to his village so that preferably he lives at the place where his agricultural farm/cattle are situated. If he works near his home, not only he gets the much needed family care and affection, but he can also better supervise and attend to his family affairs, such as kids' education and marriage, participation in the family or social functions and festivals, etc. If the place of work is near the place of his residence, he can attend to the affairs of the agriculture field/cattle on daily basis. Thus, for Haryana, where road conditions are good and villages are well connected with public transport system, the maximum preferred distance limit away from home gets naturally extended as compared to Bihar where road conditions are not so good. Figure 5.4 explains the fact that ex-servicemen of Haryana do not face much problem in finding a suitable job near their dwelling place for the simple reason that a good many districts of Haryana are directly connected with Delhi. To and fro journey for an ex-serviceman of the southern and western districts of Haryana is possible if one gets a job in Delhi. Delhi has immense opportunities for the ex-servicemen, innumerable Central Government Offices are situated there, besides the Central Secretariat. All these organisations are statutorily bound to provide reservation to the ex-servicemen. The number of reservations is more in the lower level than the upper level. It is known fact that occupational mobility (in terms of region/space) is less at the lower level of any occupation than the higher level. Therefore, it is not convenient for an ex-serviceman of Bihar to come to Delhi to work as a group D or C employee of the Central Government. For him the cost of establishment will be many times higher than the monthly income received. On the other hand, an ex-serviceman of Haryana is doubly benefited if he gets a permanent job in the Central Government in Delhi. For him whereas the extra cost of establishment remains zero as his family lives in the village, he not only earns attractive salary and facilities and the job security of the Central Government but also increases his agricultural income by putting his infrequent direct personal care and money to his land and cattle.

A great many of the ex-servicemen find a job in their own district. In every other districts in Haryana now there is a booming industrial belt. The reservation in government services, too, is pretty high. The development work in industry and services is regularly creating a great number of vacancies in the Government. Since, in all the Government vacancies, a fixed quota of jobs lie reserved for them, things become easier for the ex-servicemen of

Haryana. Vacancies kept for them are sizable and accommodate a great many of the retired armymen returning to Haryana.

The case of Bihar differs greatly from that of Haryana in terms of choice of place. Here willingness to work within the State hardly conveys the same meaning. This is not just because the size of the State is bigger and the transport communications are not so easy (time taking) but also that Bihar has at least three distinct cultural zones the North Bihar, the South Bihar (tribal plateau) and the Central Bihar. The dialects, rituals, food habits and other elements of the folk culture of these three regions sharply differ from one another. A tribal ex-serviceman of Singhbhum or Ranchi will feel a total stranger in Darbhanga than a Jat of Gurgaon in Meerut. Haryana is far more a homogeneous unit than the three cultural zones of Bihar. Cultural differences in Bihar are vivid and variety of social forces are sharpening it every day. In Bihar, it is the predominant local dialect (language) of the cultural zone which occupies a central place in everyday transactions including the urban/industrial work place, rather than Hindi. Thus, for Bihar, the choice of place is not only limited by space and time constraints but also by the cultural factor. Alien culture works as a deterrent as distance from one's place of living. Thus, it depends more on what direction an ex-serviceman in Bihar chooses from his place than merely a distance factor. The direction which leads him to a culturally familiar zone, even though more distant from the direction which leads him to culturally unfamiliar zone, will be preferable. The additional dimension of direction makes the problem of choice of work for a Bihari ex-serviceman more complex.

In the case of Bihar, the problem is further complicated in the wake of the State Government not reserving any seat in public appointments in favour of ex-servicemen. This is because the statutory quota for reservations in public appointments has already reached its limits. Transgressing the limits of reservation (50%) will be violative of the Indian Constitution. Considering the size and population of Bihar, ex-servicemen are too small a category to exert adequate political pressure for reservation. Thus, a Bihari ex-serviceman can only knock the doors of Banks and other Public Sector Undertakings of Central Government in Bihar. Thereafter, they have to accept the security jobs in private factories, business houses, etc., where they are in great demand. The last in the order of preference is a job in a security agency. A detailed treatment on regional factors influencing resettlement of ex-servicemen is being given in the next chapter. In the following sub-sections let us examine in general terms the issues involved in the organisational and job-wise preference of ex-servicemen.

Organisational Preferences: The type of organisation is another motivating factor in terms of ordering one's priority for choice of work. Army is an organisation *par excellence.* Every activity in the Army is thoroughly institutionalised, where the conformists to the organisational norms are suitably rewarded and the deviants are severely punished. Even before retirement, the armymen know well that it will be difficult to find the job security and the facilities that the Army provides when they go out. At the same time, they do not like the rigours and hazards and frequent transfers of the Army. They also do not endorse the culture of imposed subordination. The free and comparatively equalitarian life in terms of one's behaviour towards one's boss (and also towards subordinates) attracts them. Therefore, their first choice is the organisation which provides them most of the facilities which the Army gives minus its negative aspects, such as physical rigour, unstable life, deterrents of non-conformity etc. (Fig. 5.5).

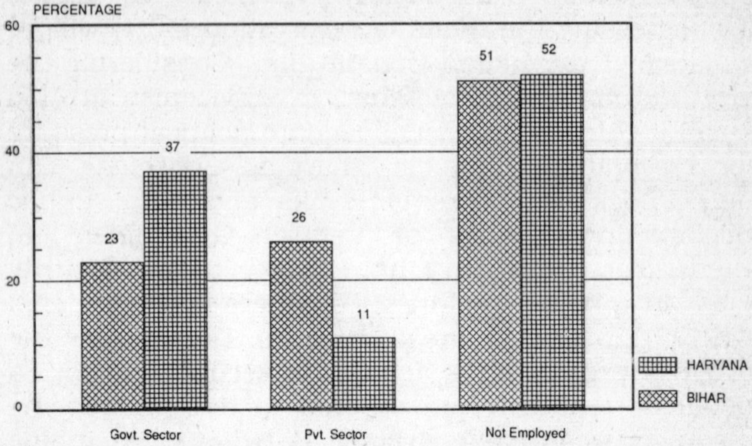

FIG. 5.5: Statewise Distribution of Employed Ex-Servicemen by Sector in which Employed

Organisationally, the security jobs in public sector banks suit them most. It offers good salary, easy facilities for loans, medical facilities and so on and so forth. Besides, the bank culture is pretty egalitarian. The security personnel in a bank is hardly supervised by an officer of security line. The duty is officially to keep standing in the shaded area/near the door, but it is sitting operationally nearly without exception. The added advantage is the posting to the village or the possibility of transfer into a nearby branch. It is a separate issue, however, whether or not the ex-servicemen meet the professional security requirement of public sector banks and other undertaking?, if yes, whether with or without additional training for the specific security requirement of a particular organisation. Although these issues are beyond the scope of present work, the researcher considers it worthwhile to place his impressions and apprehensions about the efficiency of ex-servicemen in banks and public sector undertakings as security guards.

Seldom ex-servicemen expect salary and benefits more than they drew last while in Army. Similarly, a pay package less than the amount which they received last before retirement even after adding up the pension amount is not acceptable to many of them (Fig. 5.6). Still those who work on such low salary are either incapable of getting better jobs merely by virtue of their old age or special considerations such as choice of place, work, flexibility in employment terms especially with regard to leave, agricultural income, settlement/education of the kids, etc.

Job-wise Preferences: In terms of nature of jobs preferred, the ex-servicemen are more inclined towards security jobs than any other (Fig. 5.7). The prolonged military training of giving standing sentry duty explains why most of them prefer security jobs. Non-security jobs are considered wearisome. It is also possible that the demand from the market largely for security jobs must have reinforced this attitude. But it is only because the ex-servicemen as a class are performing well in industrial security jobs that there is ready market available for their absorption. We will deliberate subsequently whether the notion that they are better security guards also on the industrial scene is correct or not.

The demand for security personnel in industrial establishments is always higher than the number of ex-servicemen getting retired every year. The ever-rising labour unrest and deteriorating law and order conditions have ensured a permanent place for this service. Apart from doing general policing function and acting as a deterrent against crime within the factory premises, they also do the additional functions of industrial safety, such as

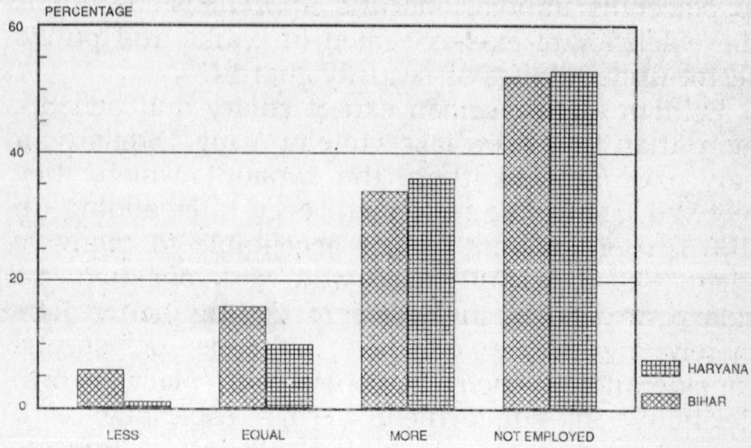

FIG. 5.6: Current Salary of Ex-Servicemen *Vice* Last Pay Drawn in Indian Army

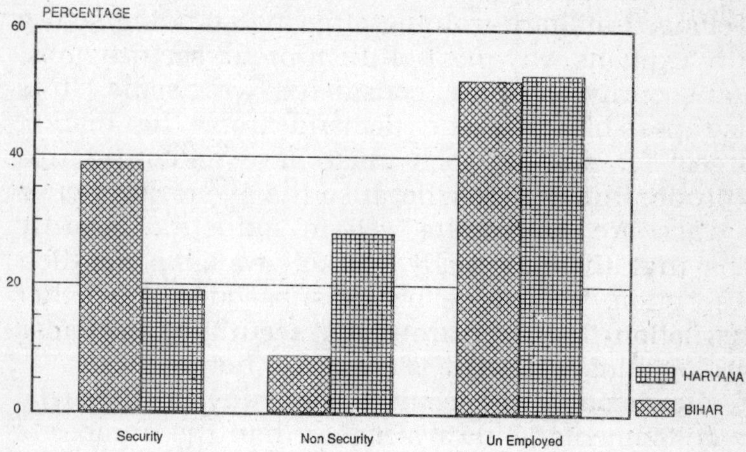

FIG. 5.7: Distribution of Employed Ex-Servicemen by Nature of Job

fire-fighting, vigilance against pilferage of raw and finished products, etc. Luckily they are also preferred by the private business houses for their smartness, discipline, health and combat skills.

Those who have their own licensed guns get an additional gun allowance of around Rs. 200 per month. But the question remains, despite their great demand why are they not available ?

Answer to this question may vary from place to place and from person to person but among the general factors contributing to their disinclination to work as a security guard in private establishment are less pay, bad work condition, hard duty and lack of job security.

Those who prefer to work in private factories as security guards, distinguish between direct employment and employment through security agencies. The latter is taken as the last option by the ex-servicemen because the principle of "agency cut" is known to them even before they join the service. Even if the agency is capable of bargaining a better deal for their services what they could have got through individual application, the popular notion (which is an outcome of the prevailing large-scale exploitation of ex-servicemen by the security agencies) prevails that the cut from their wages forms the basis of existence of security agencies. Their notion lamentably include those reputed security agencies who meet non-security and development expenditure and also earn profit through the so-called "service charges" charged in addition to the wages of the securitymen. Such expenses are ostensibly incurred largely for guaranteeing regular qualitative service to their clients. Another factor which inhibits them from joining a security agency is that most of the security agencies in India do not employ them directly but act as intermediaries to prospective employers for security personnel. Therefore, the contract of an ex-serviceman with his agency depends upon the contract of the latter with his client. Most of the agencies operating in India, organisationally as well as financially, are too small to support their security guards. Once even a small contract is cancelled, it is very difficult for a security agency to route its personnel on its own elsewhere immediately.

In Haryana, ex-servicemen are not available for private security jobs. Most of them have strong agricultural base and finding alternative employment for supplementing their income is easier. But why are the ex-servicemen not available for private security jobs also in Bihar ? We have already mentioned that Bihar Government does not provide any reservation for the employment of ex-servicemen. The agricultural base of the ex-servicemen of Bihar is also not as sound as is the case with the *Hariyanvis*. Then what possible explanation can be given for their poor response for very attractive and promising calls given by the security agencies of the State ? The fact of ex-servicemen's poor response to employment in private establishments/factories, etc., can be explained by citing an example of a company operating in Patna[2] which has very earnestly tried to attract ex-servicemen in a number of ways but has drawn almost a blank.

Organisationally, the ex-servicemen are given better terms and conditions than the young recruits. At the first place, there is age relaxation. In fact quite a few are selected ignoring even this relaxed limit. The organisation has its own rationale for keeping the overaged men. In field duty the task of supervision becomes easier because of the age factor. Heterogeneous groupings of men on duty in a security set-up of a factory further facilitates the task of an ex-serviceman in their effective supervision and administration. In spite of all the considerations, the agency finds it difficult to attract adequate number of ex-servicemen for employment.

A premier security agency of the region, therefore,

is unable to attract sufficient number of ex-servicemen even on very competitive terms. There are a few in this organisation who joined it as first try after retirement or were sponsored by the ZSBs. Even those who stuck to this organisation request for long leaves during harvesting seasons almost *en masse*. The agency being aware of this seasonal pattern keeps special arrangements to meet the short-falls either by allowing overtime or by transferring the staff from surplus to deficit areas. This shows that even in the case of Bihar, the ex-servicemen, in general, have definite agricultural income. Our data reveal that quite a few of them have acquired agricultural land even during the tenure of service. If there is no marriageable daughter at the time of retirement, investing money on land is always considered wiser than putting it in banks only on simple interest.

It is, therefore, apparent that the ex-servicemen do not prefer to work in industrial security where they are very much in demand. But what is the reason for their low absorption against reserved vacancies even among their preferred organisations such as Public Sector Banks, Public Sector Undertakings and Central Government Ministries ? In 1983, altogether 15,386 groups 'C' and 'D' posts were kept reserved by the said three Government establishments, out of which only 5,724 were filled by the ex-servicemen. Their percentage utilisations of the posts kept reserved in favour of an ex-serviceman during 1981-82 have always been below 50 per cent except in case of Central Government Ministries (in 1981) when the percentage utilisation was 56 per cent and in case of Public Sector Banks in 1983 when it went up to remarkable 70 per cent. The Public Sector Undertakings between 1981-82, however, annually reserved maximum number of vacancies out of the three major establishments. This amounted to more than 7,000 but less than 8,000 every year against Groups 'C' and 'D' posts but could never fill more than 35 per cent of the posts reserved for the ex-servicemen.[3]

While giving the reasons for shortfall in placement of ex-servicemen against their reserved vacancies, the HLC States that:

> ". . . this is because of relatively poor performance of the Sainik Board Organisation which fact was also brought to the notice of the Committee individually by ex-servicemen and associations in their memoranda and during visit of the sub-committee to the States. Besides this, there is a lack of ineffective monitoring system and poor feed-back from employers" (HLC : 1984, p.23).

With the given reservation and age, educational relaxation thereon, it is difficult to assume that any ex-serviceman will be ineligible at least for group D post. The jobs of the Central Government Organisations, as mentioned above, are centrally-advertised and the ex-servicemen are supposed to directly respond to that. If one sleeps over one's claim, no one can be held responsible to whatever he is deprived of. And ZSB is responsible for applying for the posts in favour of ex-servicemen. We have already defined resettlement as the joint responsibility of the State and the individual. If an ex-servicemen does not respond to vacancies then no agency, however efficient, can make the person (unwilling) to respond.

Whatever the criterion involved the ex-servicemen cannot be held as more deprived than the Scheduled Castes and the Scheduled Tribes. Therefore, it would have been more appropriate for the HLC to ask how many ex-servicemen were rejected from those applied against the reserved vacancies. This would have clearly revealed the actual position. Pay and allowances, perks and organisational status in public sector banks and public sector undertakings tally with each other for a given rank in their organisational structure. Then, one may ask, why have the ex-servicemen responded better for vacancies in banks than the public sector undertakings ? This reaffirms the fact that proximity to one's place of dwelling works as the most determining factor for taking up employment in majority of the cases. Banks can offer a job near ones home, but the Public Sector Undertakings may be nearer only to a few ex-servicemen. Also, work pressure and discipline in the Public Sector Undertakings is more tough than the Banks. As mentioned earlier, factors which keep an ex-serviceman bound by his place of dwelling (village) basically because he wants to compensate for his segregation with his family (basically of procreation) during his Army career are amply clear. For him, living has been compartmentalised, in one part he has done professional duties honestly; now he wants to do his family duty with the same devotion and sincerity. The additional factor (economic) is that he has agricultural land and economically productive cattle where he lives. If he leaves his place of dwelling, not only will he lose money that he may earn out of his land and cattle by its better supervision but also there is a lurcking danger of losing his 'interest' or 'possession' on his property at a time when pressure on cultivable land is increasing progressively in the same proportion the price and productivity of land is increasing.

Although apparently it is felt that the ex-servicemen are best suited for re-employment, on a deeper probing this comes to be a false notion. The reality is that even those who have sought employment, have so got it that it contributes to their interests in agricultural land and productivity. Not only that an ex-serviceman has his initial training in agriculture, he also refreshes his training and interest on his agricultural land and productivity from time to time whenever he returns to his village on leave. Thus he is seldom cut off from his roots. While in service, his sole attention is drawn towards reinforcing his root firmly rather than taking it out. For this purpose, he invests his money on the acquisition of land, or improvements in land and houses, etc.

Self-Employment: In the report of HLC, the government have made their bias explicit in favour of self-employment for the resettlement of ex-servicemen. The HLC contends that the large and medium industries have now "paved the way for the establishment of a number of small and cottage types of feeder units which are ideally suited for self-employment venture" (HLC : 1984, p.51). It has been stated – "of all opportunities available, the ex-servicemen have been chiefly attracted towards industry, agriculture and allied activities and agencies". The HLC, however, quickly adds that "owing to general lack of entrepreneurial training their efforts have not always been successful" (*Ibid.*)

It is appreciable that the Government want more job creators than job seekers. In view of the current spurt in our economy, there may as well be enough room for entrepreneurs to exploit the demand generated in various products and services. But can an ex-serviceman take up the task of an entrepreneur ? Can success in his entrepreneurial ventures be ensured if he is given adequate training? Entrepreneurship presupposes the capacity to take risk and ability to tackle uncertain and unfamiliar situations for the purpose of maintaining ones enterprise and earning profit out of it. Thus, an entrepreneur is at once an innovator and skilled manager. He is the "recipient of the non-contractual or residual income".[4]

The recruits are always caught young. Their professional training is prolonged and rigorous which is guided towards strict adherence to the orders of the superiors, physical fitness and acquisition and mastery of those skills which are necessary for performing rank role on the battle field. Job security and facilities accruing out if it are *par excellence* in Army life. Breach of duty results into court martial and punishment are severe. Expecting an entrepreneur out of an ex-serviceman goes against the vary fact that the conditioning in the Army life bears a lasting impact on an individual. The Army socialisation, in general makes a man feel economically secure, expect privileges and prestige according to his rank which are always given to him. There is hardly any room for innovativeness for the ORs and JCOs during their Army career, an element which is so indispensable for entrepreneurship. Although the officers do get opportunities to organise and manage their men and material – another element necessary for entrepreneurship – even for them, their military training hardly makes them 'the windfall absorber of the economic system . . . taking those decisions with regard to future which involvé uncertainty; and it is this political, as distinct from executive, element in the conduct of economic affairs that is entrepreneur functions *par excellence*'.[5]

Once it is demonstrable that the prolonged training acquired in Army is contrary to the entrepreneural traits, the pertinent question is, whether the elements of entrepreneurship can be injected in an armyman soon after his discharge? Any training package designed for entrepreneurship development among ex-servicemen must take into account at least four factors:

(i) an ex-serviceman is by and large product of his previous military socialisation,
(ii) the learning of entrepreneurial skills presumes unlearning age-old military training which has now become his habit,
(iii) the time which an ex-serviceman can afford for such training is limited and,
(iv) the age factor.

Even if one assumes that a training package is developed taking into consideration factors mentioned above and any other relevant factor for the purpose, it is difficult to demonstrate whether formal training plays any positive role in entrepreneurship development. The studies on entrepreneurship in India and elsewhere have failed to establish a link between entrepreneurship training and success in entrepreneurship venture. Most of the successful entrepreneurs have had no formal training in entrepreneurship. Even those who have received some formal/technical education have seldom applied their previously acquired knowledge or training in any specific sense. However, young age, urban background, experience in industry and adoption propensity have been taken as attributes positively correlated with the quality of entrepreneurship in India.[6] In another study all the entrepreneurs were persons with initiative drive and hard work, through the majority of the entrepreneurs had no technical knowledge, nor strong economic base or strong political connections.[7] Therefore, once the link between training and success itself remains unestablished, it is difficult to ensure entrepreneurial success by imparting entrepreneurial training to the ex-servicemen – a category which remains unfavourably disposed at least on two counts, viz., older age with added family responsibilities and prolonged anti-entrepreneurial military training. Even so, Government have extended certain facilities to the ex-servicemen for setting up small-scale industries which include grant of industrial plots and sheds, loans, subsidies on interest, etc.[8] Given their rural background, low educational and economic status and imposed rigorous training only for obeying the orders and command during services career, it is less likely that the JCOs and ORs, the subject-matter of the present study, will find it conducive to exploit opportunities offered by the Government for setting up their own Small Scale Industrial (SSI) units. The details of ex-servicemen having used benefits and records about the result of their venture are not known. In the present study, however, no ex-serviceman was found running his own industry nor any such scheme was under serious contemplation among anyone of them.

Another important sector for self-employment as is envisaged by the Central Government is transportation. To facilitate this the measures taken include:

(a) allotment of discarded military vehicles,
(b) grant of national permits for goods carriage, transport routes in States and tourist taxi permits and
(c) transport companies of ex-servicemen for coal transportation.

The allotment of discarded vehicles can hardly be treated as a factor facilitating viable self-employment. Though no first-hand data about the socio-economic background of the purchaser and the nature of the use of the vehicles purchased are available, it has been gathered that only a few

JCOs and ORs have received such vehicles so far. Even those who have received them have hardly put them to some regular remunerative/productive use. Although the transfer of ownership of vehicles is legally barred for three years, it is said that informal licence for using the vehicle is soon given to those who can pay enough consideration for it and actual transfer of ownership takes place automatically after three years. Even if one assumes, however, that an allottee at last gets an opportunity to put the purchased vehicle into productive use, number of such vehicles disposed are too small to significantly alter the state of self-employment prospects of ex-servicemen as a major alternative to their re-settlement as against re-employment. Average figure of vehicles disposed of between 1981-83 is 781. In view of 70,000 ex-servicemen being added to the existing population every year, only one out of ninety can have a chance to get such vehicle if individuals, retired previously, do not compete for the same. With regard to national permits, the HLC states:

> ". . . the Ministry of Transport and Shipping . . . had issued instruction to all State Governments to reserve 10 per cent of the National permits in favour of ex-servicemen. The secretaries of the respective Rajya Sainik Boards are expected to follow this up with the State Governments and ensure that these instructions are implemented, *provided ex-servicemen of the area seek such benefits*" (HCL 1984: p.52, emphasis added).

Although driving in the far remote area has been a familiar job for all MT drivers in the Army, it is not known how many of the ex-servicemen and how many of the MT drivers among them have availed of such opportunities. It is also not known how many of the permit owners are actually utilising the permits as entrepreneurs and how many permit have a property value capable of being informally rented or sold. Although it is not justified to make any remark without having special knowledge of subject, one can of course say that most of the statutory provisions to give special assistance to a class of people for the purpose of doing their own business have either failed or have been greatly diluted by vested interests.[9] There are no complaints about the provision for reservation in favour of ex-servicemen. It is apprehended that, being devoid of any entrepreneurial trait, many of them may not succeed in their business venture and the benefits specially meant for them may be enjoyed by others.

These days there is great profit in transportation of coal. The income is assured as the services are hired by a single client. For more enterprising transporters (and in coal transport it is nearly impossible for the less adventurous to survive) there is good profit also between loading and unloading. The business is so notorious for the invincible influence of the mafia and it is impossible to believe that the ex-servicemen have remained unaffected from the clutches of the mafia and that the benefits accuring is going in the right hands.

Another important sector for self-employment as envisaged by the Government is agriculture. The findings of the present study also suggest that most of the self-employed ex-servicemen are engaged in the agriculture sector (Fig. 5.8). The DGR provides 'guidance in the field of various agro-industries, viz., Diary Farming, Poultry, Piggery, Sheep and Goat Breeding, Bee-keeping, Sericulture, etc. Rajya Sainik Boards are, therefore, requested to provide necessary guidance to the interested parties in their area of operation. This is one sector where ex-servicemen have performed well in general, most of them even without seeking any guidance or financial assistance from any other source. Reasons are manifold which ensure their success in agro-industrial venture, provided they are willing to take up the task whole-heartedly. Most of the interviewees, however, took up agriculture only as a second option, either in case no employment was available to them or the available employment did not engage them fully.

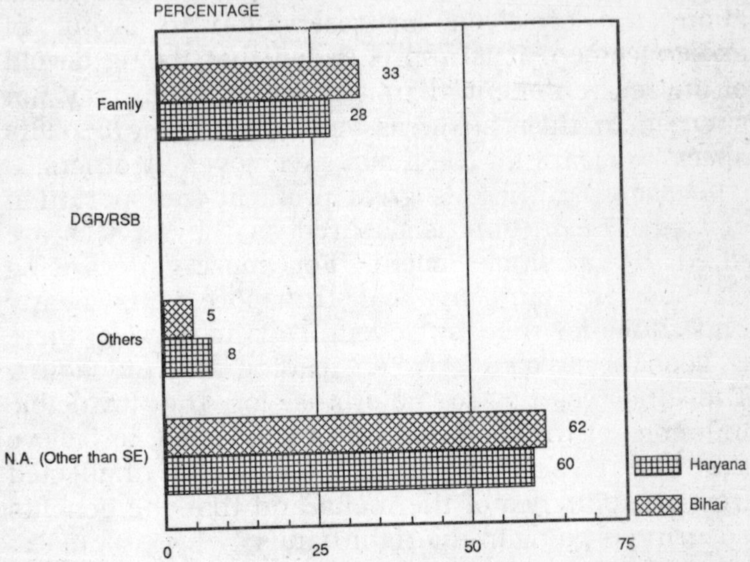

FIG. 5.8: Nature of Self-Employment

For the successful ones, it was found that only clarity of goal and firm will were the crucial factors. Neither training nor financial assistance was found necessary. This is because most of the ex-servicemen have agricultural background. They have worked in the field, ploughed the land and reared the cattle. They are also aware of the socio-economic environments of their villages. They have seldom been out of touch from agricultural activities. While in services majority of the ex-servicemen having some agricultural land regularly visit their countryside also to demonstrate and maintain right to their ancestral property. During their service tenure, the family land and agriculture invariably get benefited from their regular contribution. Thus, the contact of an armyman with his land and agriculture is maintained throughout both in terms of regular remittances for the purpose of agriculture and also in terms of his active and physical participation in agriculture activities for about two months in every year when he visits home on leave. Even while on duty in the Army, quite a few have to work in the military farms, look after the cattle, etc. Therefore, no break in their initial interest, training or familiarity towards their agricultural activities takes place.

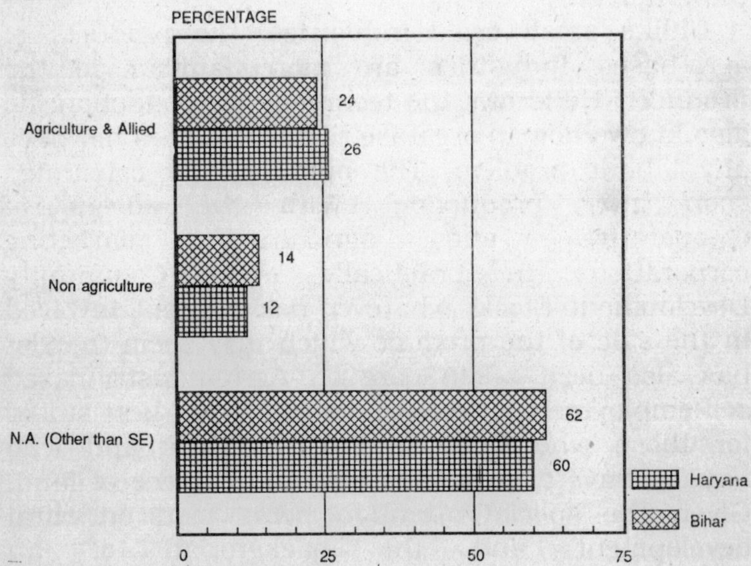

FIG. 5.9: Prime Motivator of Self-Employment

It is evident from Fig. 5.9 that the self-employed ex-servicemen received primary motivation for their current self-employment venture through their family background. It may be noted, though lamentably, that none of the self-employed ex-serviceman from Bihar or Haryana preferred to name the DGR/RSB as prime motivator for their current self-employment venture out of the options given. The responses of the ex-servicemen may not have direct correlation with the quality of work being done by the Self-Employment Directorate of the DGR. But it does indicate the need for streamlining the functioning of the directorate so that it receives better appreciation of its beneficiaries.

The investments required for the agro-industries are little. The household equipments and members of the family are assets for any new work undertaken. The agro-industries go hand in hand with (the face to face, personal relationship) the type of relationship characteristic of the villages. Everything is within the conceivable limit of the undertaker.

Unlike small scale industries, the products of agro-based industries are more familiar to the producer. He knows the technique of production, he also knows how to organise things. He does not have any labour problem. The produce gets consumed soon after production. With the advent of co-operatives and agricultural marketing corporations in practically every Community Development Block, whatever risk element involved in the sale of the produce which may seem to exist has also been taken care of. Agro-industry-based self-employment, therefore, is an activity best suited for those who came from rural areas and who usually have a small dwelling and a piece of land. Given the special attention being paid on rural development and the background of an ex-serviceman who returns to his village with a decent lump sum amount after retirement, it is easier and lucrative to stick to the village and make agriculture a source of high livelihood for the remaining part of his life. He does not have to handle an unfamiliar member or an uncertain situation, like in industry and transport. Favourable result in any of the agro-industrial venture is almost assured. What is required for this is his will to take up the task, to understand that he can earn more in agro-industry than in petty employment. The military training of hard work and discipline, if properly translated into any agro-industrial venture is bound to bring good fortune to them. After retirement, an ex-serviceman wants to lead a peaceful life. He is happy after getting freed from age-old rigorous routine duties and tight subordination. He loves freedom and relaxation of post-retired life and would not normally compromise with it, unless it is inevitable to do so. Therefore, in agro-industry, an ex-serviceman finds all that he wants. This is a unique gratifying job-experience for an ex-serviceman where job satisfaction, social prestige and monetary rewards all combine together.

In addition, regular allotment of Massy-Ferguson tractors in small numbers also helps the ex-servicemen, particularly those having larger landholding of the agriculturally-developed regions. Since the number of such allotments is small, their impact is very limited. For example, between 1981-83 a total of 492 tractors were distributed in 11 agriculturally-advanced States. However, three States have claimed the bulk of them (461 tractors), namely, Rajasthan (322), Haryana (77) and Punjab (62) [See Appendix T of HLC Report, p. 135].

Agencies, including the allotment of booths and stalls, become another avenue for the self-employment of ex-servicemen. This goes very well with their urge to earn money with regulated and assured system of work, where risk is practically nil and at the same time there is charm of freedom and independence.

The Food Corporation of India (FCI), Hindustan Fertiliser Corporation (HFC), Rashtriya Chemical Fertilisers (RCF) and National Fertilisers Ltd. (NFL) have reserved 15 per cent of their fertiliser agencies for allotment to ex-servicemen. This is one package which goes hand in hand with the other packages available for self-employment in agriculture and agro-based industries. Fertiliser agency is quite remunerative these days and also easier for an ex-serviceman to handle without any special training because the functions are simple and the results of one's labour are predictable.

There were 548 *Jai Jawan* Stalls as on 9 December, 1983 run by ex-servicemen throughout India (the Statewise position is given in Appendix 'U' of the HLC Report 1984, p.136). "While the sites are obtained from the Municipal Authorities concerned, the structures are generally built by various commercial companies such as, Pure Drinks, Modern Bakeries, etc." (DGR:1984, p.80). It is a scheme which is very much in tune with the likings and limitations of ex-servicemen desirous of getting settled in urban areas.

"The milk vending booths of the Mother Dairy in Delhi are manned by ex-service personnel. There are 300 such booths in Delhi. The Delhi Milk Supply Scheme has also appointed 30 ex-servicemen as concessionaires at their milk vending booths" (HLC:1984, p.52). Although this scheme is limited within the city of Delhi, it is very much in line with the *Jai Jawan* stall type of activity. Agency of any kind suits ex-servicemen. They are happier here because of the factors already mentioned. With the active utilisation of ex-servicemen in the public distribution system, which spans in every nook and corner of the country, their re-settlement should not be a problem.

Among the self-employment avenues, for the ORs

and JCOs, therefore, agriculture and agro-industries should be encouraged. They should be made an integral part of the public distribution system and agencies for the retail outlets of the goods produced by the Government may be granted to them on priority basis. All these will be in tune with their job preferences, attitudes and ability and will go long way in coping with their problems of re-settlement. By involving them into public distribution system, most of them are likely to get a self-employment avenue at the place of their dwelling and this would instantly facilitate their re-settlement.

A brief discussion on the process and patterns of re-settlement of ex-servicemen whether by way of re-employment or self-employment suggests that their problems are of a different nature from those of either the fresh competitors in the labour market or the duly retired civilians having completely withdrawn from active economic life. That is, the story of ex-serviceman is rather different. While in services they are away from home, therefore, are very much in demand when they occasionally visit home on leave. Once they come finally to live with their family members, they come with an altogether different status. Now they are retired. There is loss both in terms of money and position. Whereas the expectations of family and relatives are on the increasing side, they confront a typically anomic situation both in terms of time and money. They are suddenly thrown out from a tight work schedule to an idle living. Soon people start saying "Why don't you work ?" But there is no work for them at home. Moreover, an ex-serviceman is habitually not used to entertaining petty family bickerings and complaints because for most of his service tenure he has been physically away from his family. All this frustrates him. His family members, too, are not used to day-to-day interferences by him. His wife and children grunt on his excessive interferences in family matters. Thus, soon after retirement he faces social, economic and cultural voids. He feels he is no longer useful to others. His self-hatred at times gets transmuted into hatred for society at large about which every social planner should be cautioned.

We will discuss more about the sociological factors influencing re-settlement of ex-servicemen in the coming chapters. What we have suggested in this chapter is that the ex-servicemen's problems are of special nature and, therefore, deserve special treatment from every corner. The re-settlement patterns have shown that efforts both on the part of society and the State are commendable. Further, their lack of entrepreneurial capacity and every attempt to subordinate the interest of the second employment below family and agricultural requirements only go to prove that their problems are of a different nature and ought to be tackled differently. An employment near his village or self-employment based on or contributing to his agricultural activities best suits him. There are hosts of developmental programmes, at district and block levels, including IRDP, NREP etc., in which room can always be found for the active participation and utilisation of ex-servicemen. In addition, as already suggested, they can play a key role in the public distribution system and in the handling of the agencies of the consumer goods being produced by the Government.

NOTES

1. For example, Himachal Pradesh and Punjab have reserved 15 per cent of posts of all category for the ex-servicemen. Haryana reserves 5 per cent of Class I and II posts and 17 per cent each for class III and IV posts for ex-servicemen. Please see para 12.2 and Appendix 'X' of the HLC Report,

1984, GOI., pp-153-7 for further details.

2. The institutional case study refers to M/s Security and Intelligence Services, B. Bagaicha, Dak-Bunglow Road, Patna - 800 001. The professionally managed agency employs over 2,500 men to cater to the safety and security needs of various types of industries. Although ex-servicemen form very small proportion of its total manpower, most of the ex-servicemen are either used as supervisors or Officer-in-Command on field duties, or as Trainers/Training Officers at its Cadet Training Centre, located at Balchampa in Palamau District, Bihar.
3. Data worked out on the basis of Appendix 'P' of HLC, 1984, p. 131.
4. Maurice Dobb, *Encyclopaedia of the Social Sciences*, Vol. 5, New York, 1948, p. 559.
5. *Ibid.*, p. 559.
6. *SIET: Socio-Psychological Factors Influencing the Adoption of the Innovation of Starting A Small Industry Unit - A Research Study*, 1974, SIET Institute, Hyderabad. The study of 61 entrepreneurs near Hyderabad has been reviewed by M.V. Deshpande, *Entrepreneurship of Small Scale Industries*, New Delhi, 1982, p. 71.
7. Gaikwad, V.R. and R.N. Tripathi, *Socio-Psychological Factors Influencing Entrepreneurship in Rural Areas*, National Institute of Community Development, Hyderabad, 1970. It attempts at bringing out the pre-requisites of successful entrepreneurship by studying the small entrepreneurs of Tanku region of West Godavari District. Also reviewed by Deshpande, *op. cit.*, p. 70.
8. Refer Appendices P & Q of HLC Report, G.O.I., 1984. In a booklet, entitled *Ex-Serviceman as Entrepreneur 1981*, DGR, 843 items reserved for small scale industries have been listed out of which 384 items are kept reserved for exclusive purchase by the Government from the small scale sector.
9. For example, a few years back the Bihar Government, by a notification, made qualified engineers as the only eligible category for getting Government contract because in those days political pressures by the unemployed engineers had gathered momentum. The provision did not bring about any change, the old contractors continued to get contracts in the name of unemployed qualified engineers, some of them even in the direct employment of such contractors.

6

FACTORS INFLUENCING RE-SETTLEMENT: Time and Region

TIME IS the best healer. With time circumstances, priorities and significance of a problem change. But it is seldom that time passes without an activity. It is not just the time that heals but various activities – acts of comission and ommission – taking place and inter-playing with each other in a given time that brings about the healing effect.

The main purpose of man's activities have been maximisation of pleasure and reduction of pain through stability and peace in one's life. The purpose of one's life is best served, however, through collective living and finding its full expression in social relationships. Re-settlement as a process is also guided towards this ultimate purpose of mankind, the applicability of which is limited to those who are governed by the conditions of re-settlement in a particular socio-historical context. (See Chapter 1).

Time plays a crucial role in re-settlement process as it determines whole sets of activities in given social choices for all those who retire prematurely in a particular age-group. Further, from therapeutic viewpoint too, a time limit is implicitly set for the re-settlement of the ex-Servicemen retiring in a particular year within which their problems are either solved or get transmuted and no longer remain a subject- matter of re-settlement. Thus, both nature of the problems of the ex-servicemen and its plausible solutions are temporally determined. We have already discussed in earlier chapters the importance of time factor in determining nature of the problems of ex-servicemen. In this chapter, it is intended to assess the significance of time factor affecting re-settlement of ex-servicemen. Subsequently, regional factors influencing re-settlement of ex-servicemen will be discussed. Rank and caste are the two important sociological factors influencing the quality of re-settlement of ex-servicemen in India. These two factors have been dealt with separately in Chapter 7.

Year of Retirement as a Factor Influencing Re-settlement

The analysis of data clearly shows that the ex-servicemen retired in 1985 are less "re-settled" than those retiring in the preceding years. This factor has shown its significance independent of the regional and sociological factors being dealt with subsequently. It is also implied in the discussion that the process of re-settlement has a definite time cycle. It begins from the void created on the date of retirement/release and has a tendency to maintain the socio-economic equilibrium of pre-retired life. Till the equilibrium is re-established, the ex-servicemen live in an anomic situation and, therefore, they struggle for re-settlement.

One of the chief indicators of re-settlement is seeking second career after retirement whether by way of re-employment or self-employment. This not only provides an ex-serviceman with the urgently required economic status and associated perks and privileges but also gives him enough justification to stay away from the day-to-day affairs of the family at least for some limited hours every day. Once an ex-serviceman returns to his family permanently, he finds a difference in the attitude and behaviour of his wife, kids and relatives, though expressed in subtle manner. The difference of attitude gets clearer when he compares it with his previous visits to home on holidays for short durations. Therefore, re-employment or self-employment becomes necessary not only to meet the rising economic demand of the family members in the wake of sharply slumped pensionary income but also that he wants to get liberated from the situation that has compelled him to sit idly in the family day and night. Those who fail to get re-settled in a socially desirable manner (i.e., by way of employment or self-employment), soon find some other ways to be absent from the family which ranges from whiling away time in stray gossip, playing cards and alcoholism to delinquent and other socially disapproved activities.

Therefore, in terms of employability, data presented in Figs. 6.1(a) and 6.1(b) show that out of the total number of ex-servicemen interviewed for the year 1985, 45 per cent from Bihar and 50 per cent from Haryana were unemployed. The corresponding figure of the preceding years, i.e., for 1984, 1983, 1982 and 1981, are 11.1 per cent, 10 per cent, 9.1 per cent and zero per cent for Bihar and 10 per cent, zero per cent, zero per cent and zero per cent for Haryana, respectively. This proves that there is a defined time-limit within which an ex-serviceman is employed/self-employed or is not at all. The data from the field also indicate that most of the ex-servicemen from Bihar and Haryana got fixed up within a year's time. Those finding their first job in two to three, three to four and four to five years after retirement are one per cent each in case of Bihar. In Haryana, none could find his first job as later as after three to four and four to five years of his retirement. Such as Bihar, only one per cent of the total ex-servicemen interviewed in Haryana showed that they got their first job between two to three years after their retirement.

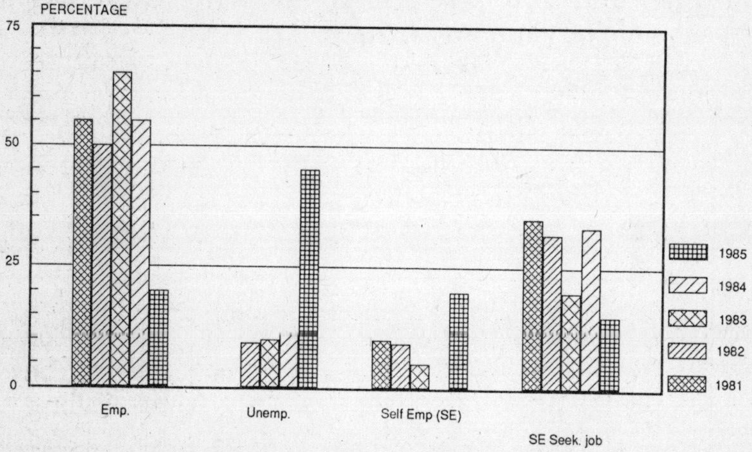

FIG. 6.1(a): Occupatitonal Status of Ex-Servicemen by Year of Retirement: Bihar

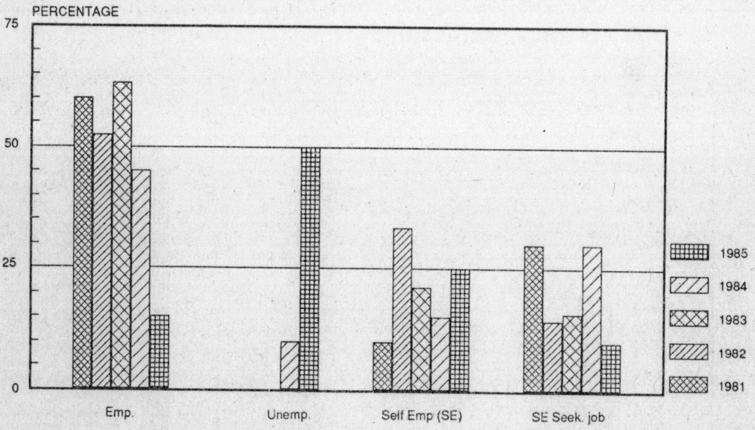

FIG. 6.1(b): Occupational Status of Ex-Servicemen by year of Retirement: Haryana

It is significant to note that none retiring in the

year 1981 from both the States were found unemployed. Similarly, for those retiring in 1982, 1983 and 1984, the level of unemployment for each year was 9, 10 and 11 per cent, respectively, in case of Bihar and zero, zero and 10 per cent, respectively, in case of Haryana Fig. 6.2(a & b).

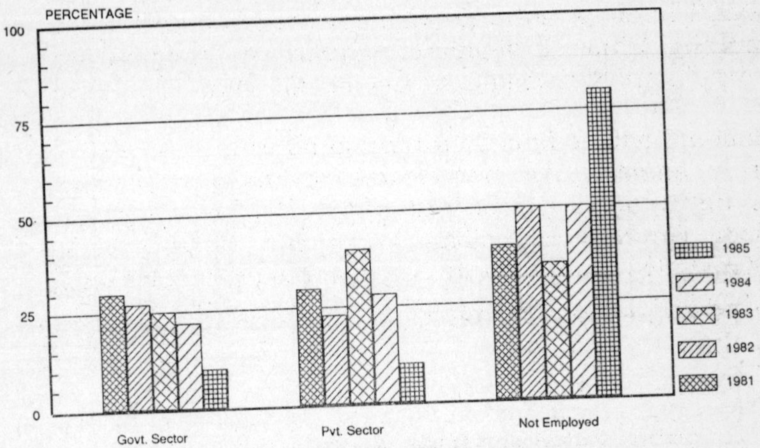

FIG. 6.2(a): Sectorwise Employment of Ex-Servicemen by Year of Retirement: Bihar

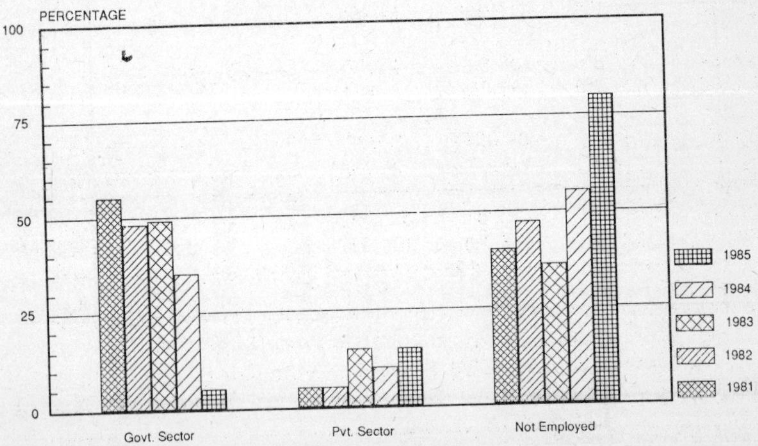

FIG. 6.2(b): Sectorwise Employment of Ex-servicemen by Year of Retirement: Haryana

In terms of quality of employment also, the gap after retirement has shown its significance. The first preference of ex-servicemen in terms of organisation is Government job so that they may enjoy the job security and some other privileges of the kind already enjoyed before retirement. But for all Government posts there is keen competition. Moreover, recruitment process in the Government is time-taking. Therefore, the normal course of re-employment for the majority of ex-servicemen is to get whatever they find first and then try for a change.

The analysis of data indicates that none retiring in 1985 had a Central Government job either in Bihar or in Haryana. Similarly, in terms of pay and perks none retiring in 1985 from Bihar got more than the pre-retired salary, whereas from Haryana five per cent of those retiring in the same year could get higher above Rs 100 but lower below Rs 500 than the pre-retired period. The facts are presented in Fig. 6.3(a) and Fig. 6.3(b).

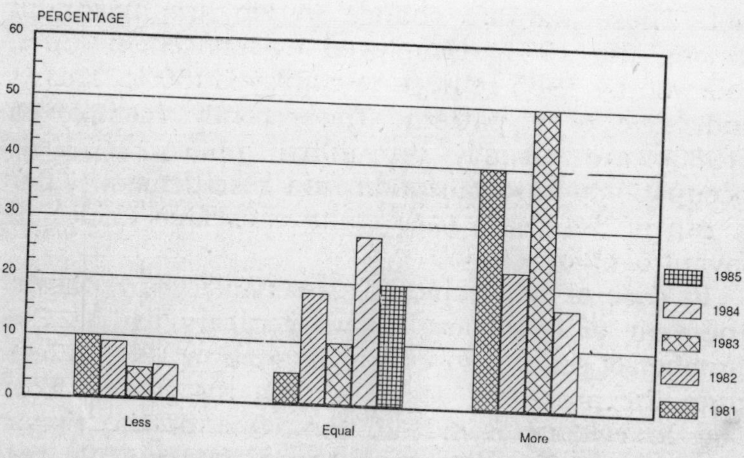

FIG. 6.3(a): Current Salary of Ex-Servicemen *vice* Last Pay Drawn in Indian Army and by Year of Retirement: Bihar

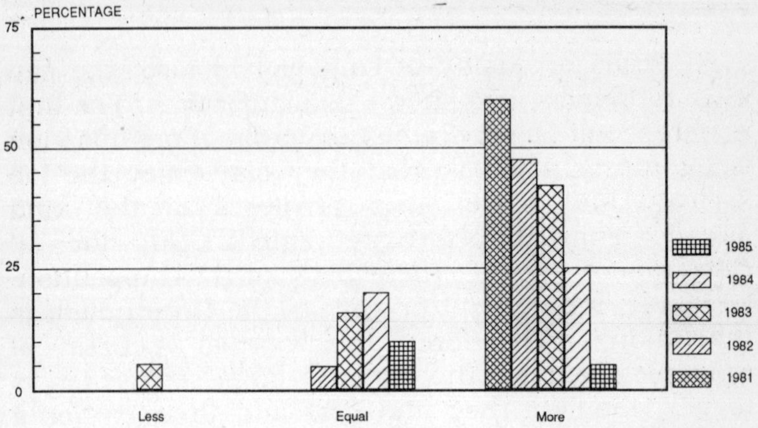

FIG. 6.3(b): Current Salary of Ex-Servicemen *vice* Last Pay Drawn in Indian Army and by Year of Retirement: Haryana

Whether one wants to change one's job or not is also one of the indicators to find out if one has compromised with one's initial job. However, the fact may not necessarily indicate whether one is satisfied with one's job or not. One of the questions asked was whether one has applied for some better job or not. Those wanting change in job are maximum among the 1981 reemployed ex-servicemen (60%) followed by 1985 retirees re-employed (50%). This is indicative of a pattern. The recently reemployed (1985) are usually in initial phase of their occupational resocialization and resettlement. After a gap of 3-4 years they make conscious choice in favour of change in job.

In case of self-employed ex-servicemen, however, the year of retirement shows contrary result. The number of self-employed wanting job in 1985 is less than the preceding years in both the States. This fact is evident from Fig. 6.4. One of the major explanations for this tendency is that initially the ex-servicemen are geared up to take up self-employment ventures but after some time they find it for themselves difficult to cope up with a number of factors which are to be inevitably managed to make any profit earning venture successful.

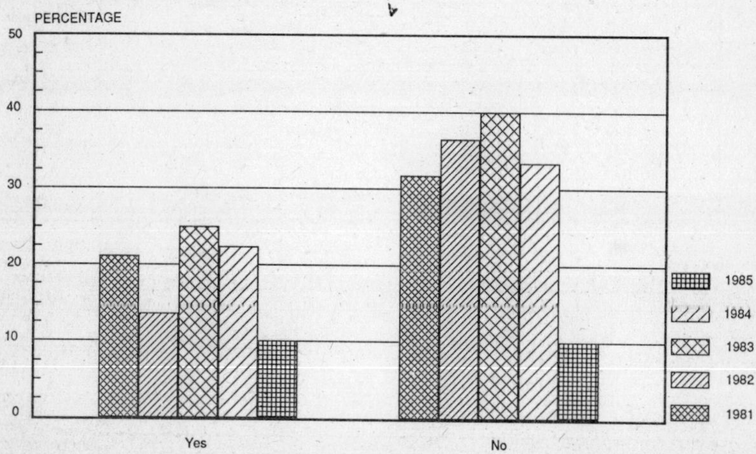

FIG. 6.4: **Employed Ex-servicemen Seeking Better Jobs by Year of Retirement (Bihar and Haryana)**

Another indicator also proves the fact that the recently retired ex-servicemen are not as re-settled as the ex-servicemen retired two to three years earlier from the time the fieldwork was conducted. The ex-servicemen were asked to choose one of the positive effects of retirement. Most of the ex-servicemen interviewed in both the States provided some or other reasons of positive effects of their retirement. But some of the respondents saw no positive effect of retirement.

As it is apparent from Figs. 6.5(a) and 6.5(b) that those replying in the negative decrease from 1985 onwards if the figures for 1981 of Bihar are ignored. The quick decrease in the negative response of those replying in the negative from among the retirees from 1984 onwards in case of Haryana proves the fact of quick and qualitatively better resettlement of ex-servicemen in the State.

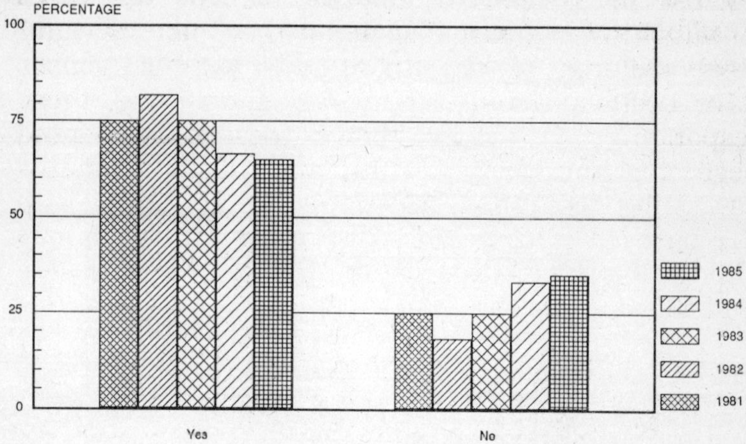

FIG. 6.5(a): Positive Effects of Retirement by Year of Retirement: Bihar

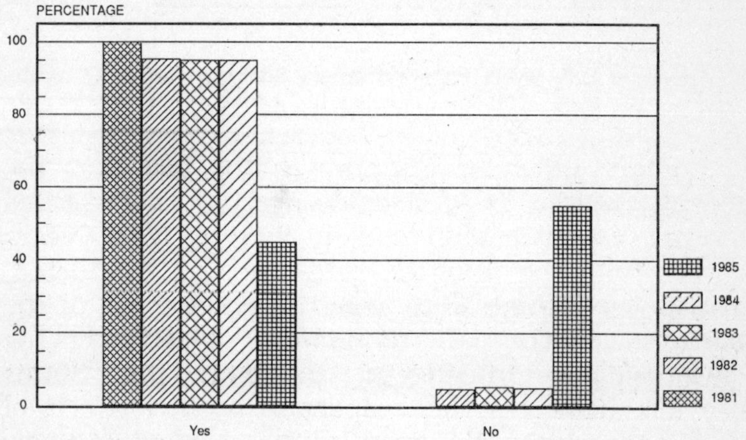

FIG. 6.5(b): Positive Effects of Retirement by Year of Retirement: Haryana

Clarity or otherwise of the ex-serviceman regarding the size of his family is also one of the indicators suggesting whether he has attained stability in life or not. It is interesting to note that only 17 per cent of the respondents from Bihar and 11 per cent from Haryana have reported that they do not use any family planning method. However, when it was further probed whether they plan to have more children or not, more interesting responses have been gathered. Figure 6.6 shows that those responding as "none" have descending trend beginning from the year 1981 and those responding as "undecided" show ascending trend. Thus, with the passage of time the issue regarding the family size gets settled and, gradually, one remains less undecided about the issue.

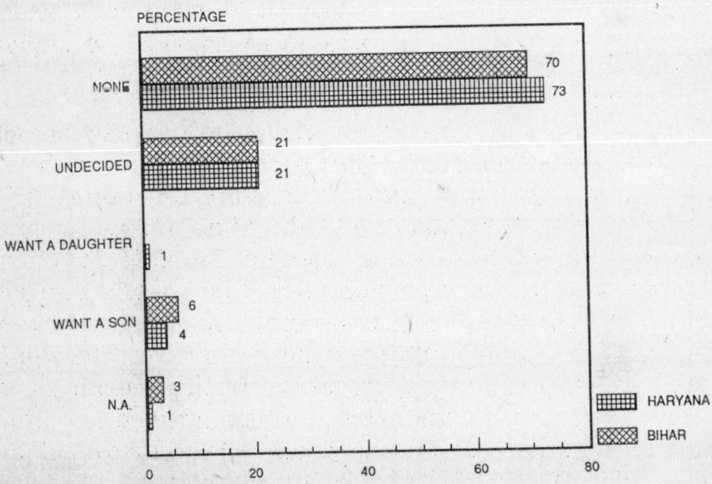

FIG. 6.6: Ex-servicemen Planning – More children

A question was put to the respondents as to how they felt after retirement in comparison with their tenure during the Indian Army. Year of retirement has shown direct significance in terms of one's retired life ratings *vice* pre-retired life, as is evident from Fig. 6.7(a) and 6.7(b). For example, those responding that they felt worse after retirement are maximum from among the retirees of 1985 from both the States. The trend gradually decreases up to 1983 in case of Bihar and upto 1984 in case of Haryana with marginally increasing trend for the

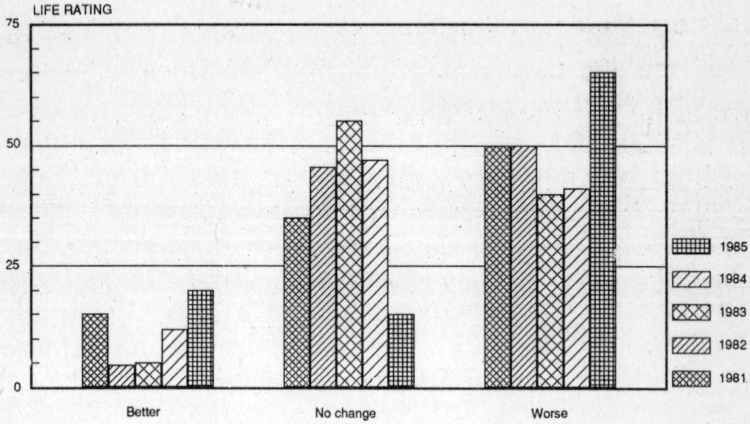

FIG. 6.7(a): Self-Rating of Ex-Servicemen *vice* Pre-retired Life and by Year of Retirement: Bihar

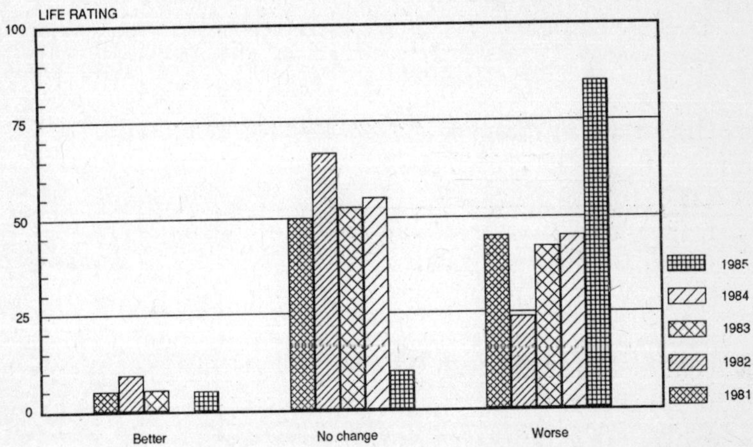

FIG. 6.7(b): Self-Rating of Ex-Servicemen *vice* Pre-retired Life and by Year of Retirement: Haryana

preceding years. The trend gets confirmed when we examine the responses "no change" from both the States. Whereas maximum 1985 retirees rated their retired life as worse, minimum retiring from the same year thought that there was no change between retired and pre-retired life. The response "no change" has ascending trend up to 1983 in case of Bihar and up to 1984 in case of Haryana. The discrepancy in results of response "better", however, requires some further explanations. A large number of JCOs retiring in the year 1985 felt better after retirement which was not so in case of Haryana for the corresponding year.

It is, therefore, evident that year of retirement is an important factor in the analysis of issues relating to re-settlement of ex-servicemen. All the figures mentioned in Figs. 6.1 to 6.7 clearly indicate that the difference between 1984 and 1985 is much more marked than any two adjoining years, i.e. 1981-82, or 1982-83, or 1983-84. More stable responses appear from 1984 downward. Therefore, it can be said that it takes about 12 to 18 months for an ex-serviceman to get re-settled from the date he retires.

Regional Factors Influencing Re-settlement

Like time, space is also one of the major factors influencing various processes which guides the activities of human beings. A region has a territorial boundary the salient features of which are usually defined by its historicity, language and culture. A region is also defined in terms of levels of development or on grounds of political and administrative expediency. The level of development of a particular region necessarily determines the extent, type and nature of employment situation in the region. Since the major thrust of re-settlement is on re-employment or self-employment of ex-servicemen, we will quickly dwell upon some of the distinguished features of the levels of development of the two States under the present study, namely, Bihar and Haryana. This is not to say that the history, language, culture or politico-administrative set-up of the two States are irrelevant or absolutely insignificant in the context of the re-settlement process. Wherever these regional factors are significant, we will discuss them in our analysis. However, presently we will discuss the situation in the two States are placed ignoring internal differences.

Some salient features about the uneven economic development of the two States are being discussed here in brief in order to make proper appraisal and evaluation of regional factors on the re-settlement of ex-servicemen in India. All the figures mentioned here have been carefully culled down from *A Social and Economic Atlas of India* (Oxford, 1987).

There are various factors which suggest that Haryana is economically far more developed than Bihar. Higher level of economic development means more jobs and better wages for those living in the State. In 1984-85, against all-India average of 36.90 per cent, Bihar had 47.87 per cent of its population below poverty line whereas in Haryana it was only 17.02 per cent (Fig. 6.8). Against all-India per capita annual income from agriculture and industry for the year 1981-82 which accounted for Rs.834, it was Rs.1,327 in case of Haryana and only Rs.612 in case of Bihar. Similarly, in 1981 the agricultural workers in Bihar, both male and female, were in greater proportion than the all-India figure. In case of Haryana, however, the agricultural workers were far less in number than the all-India average. In 1981, 19.6 per cent of male and 42.2 per cent of female workers of their respective workforce were engaged in agriculture in India. The corresponding figures in case of Bihar were 30.6 per cent (M) and 63.3 per cent (F) and in case of Haryana it was only 15.6 per cent (M) and 22.0 per cent (F). This shows how great is the pressure on agriculture in Bihar and how less is it in Haryana. In terms of overall population density, too, Haryana showed much lesser density of population per square kilometre in 1981 than Bihar though the density of population of Haryana was slightly more than the all-India average for the same year. The density of population per square kilometre in 1981 for India, Bihar and Haryana were 208, 402 and 292, respectively.

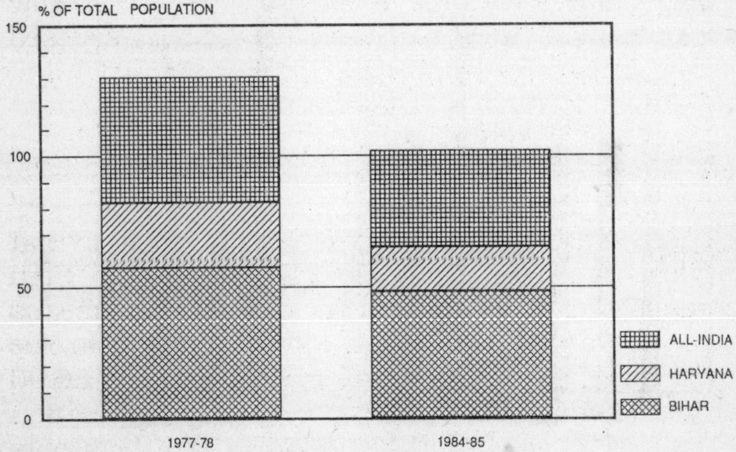

FIG. 6.8: **Population Below Poverty Line**

All these figures suggest that in Bihar the number of persons working in agriculture and unorganised sector is proportionately greater. Poverty in Bihar is rampant and job prospects are very bleak. Pressure on land in the State forces people to move out of the State in search of livelihood. Heavy dependence of working force on agriculture is one of the main indicators of under-development. Similarly, lesser percentage of employed workers in the total main workers is also one of the indicators of under-development which is far less [20.3 per cent (M), 8.4 per cent (F)] in case of Bihar and much greater in case of Haryana [33.6 per cent (M), 16.0 per cent (F)].

Development of a region is also ascertained on the basis of the degree of non-working population and availability of minimum needs, education and health, communication facilities, etc. in society. Figures 6.9 to 6.11(e) amply prove the point on every count that Haryana is far more developed than Bihar.

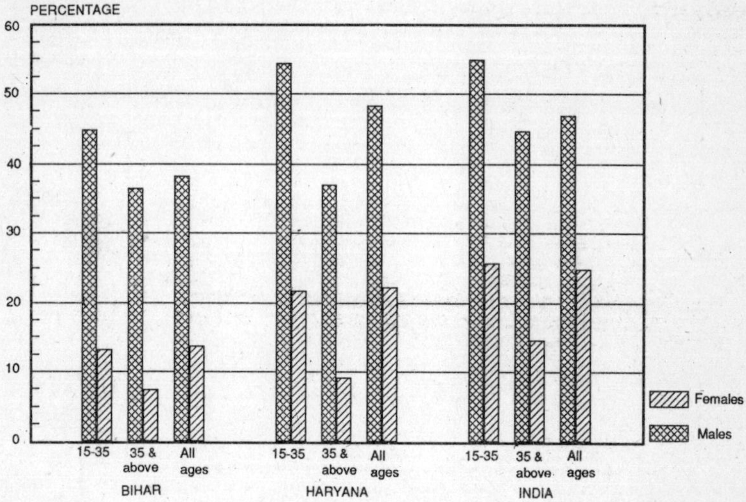

FIG. 6.9: Literates by Age-groups

Against the backdrop of these data and on the basis of field data to be presented, it is now intended to discuss the nature of relationship between the economic development of a particular region and its impact on the re-settlement of ex-servicemen. Our discussion also takes into account history, culture, political and administrative situations of the two States, although briefly.

In terms of occupational status, apparently there is not much difference between Bihar and Haryana. There were 15 per cent unemployed ex-servicemen in Bihar and 12 per cent in Haryana. Those reported as employed were more in Bihar (49%) than in Haryana (47.%). The difference, however, is clear when we take into consideration the quality of employment or self-employment provided in the two States in relation to total material output or benefit

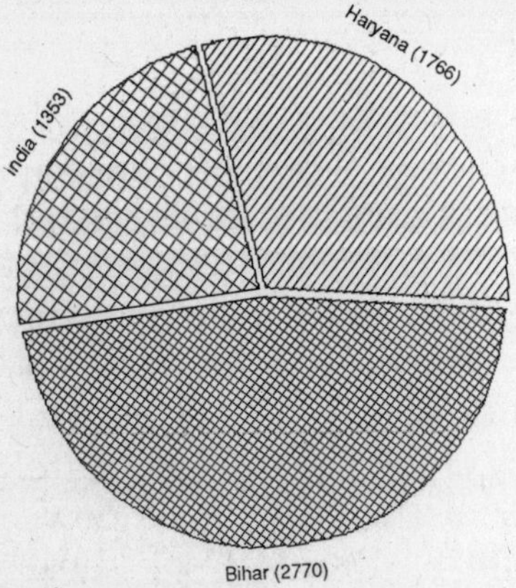

FIG. 6.10: Number of Persons per Hospital and Dispensary Beds, 1985

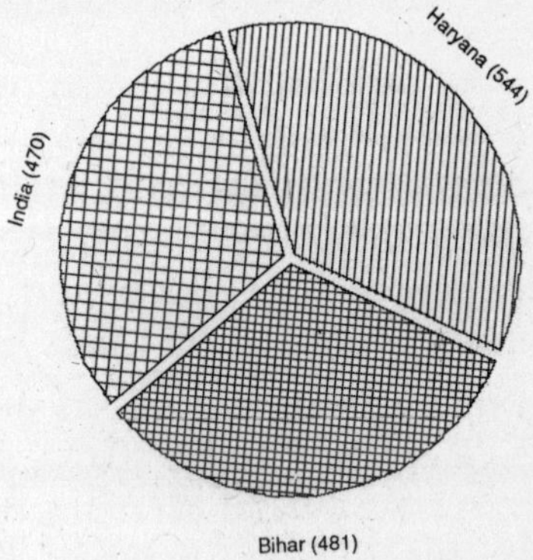

FIG. 6.11(a): Communication: Road Length per 1000 sq. km, 1981-82

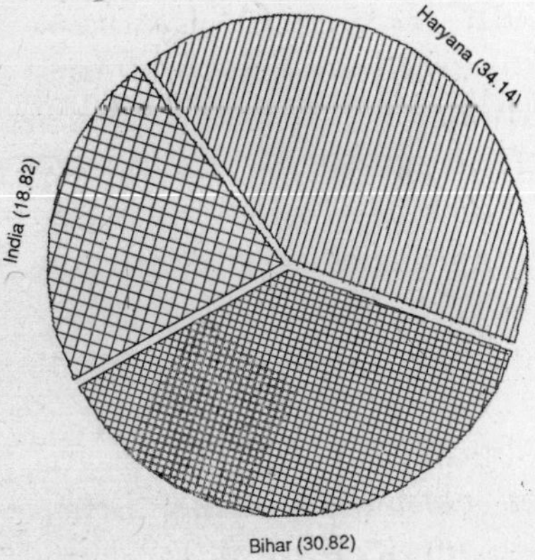

FIG. 6.11(b): Communication: Railway Route per 1000 sq. km, 1981-82

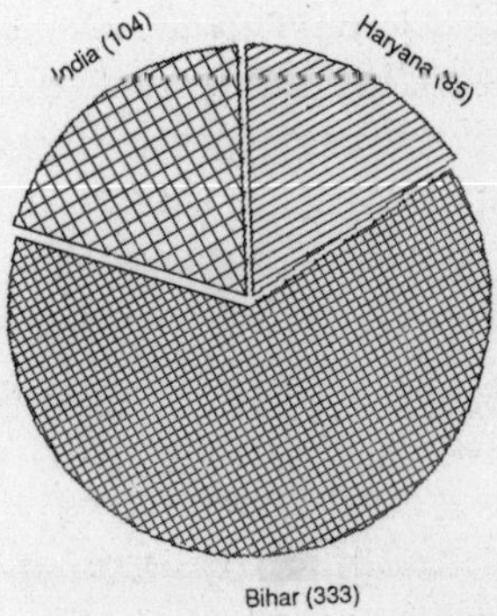

FIG. 6.11(c): Communication: Number of Persons Per Registered Motor Vehicle, 1982-83

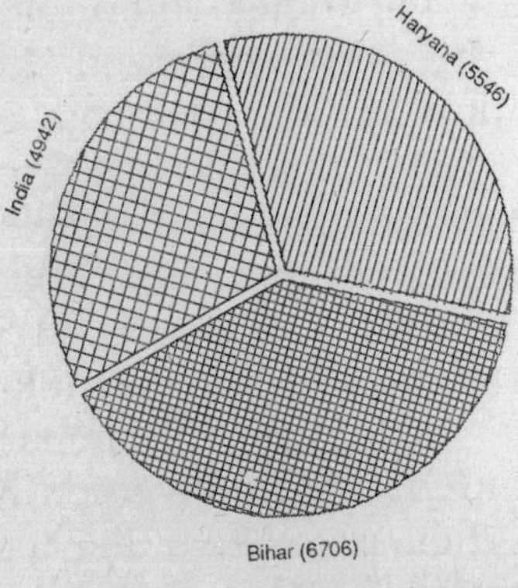

FIG. 6.11(d): Communication: Number of Persons Per Post Office, 1983-84

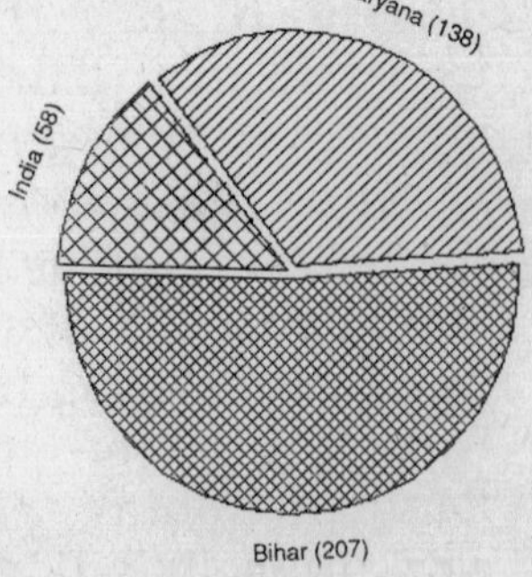

FIG. 6.11(e): Number of Persons Per Cinema House (in thousands), 1985-86

accruing from the second career occupation of the ex-servicemen and their socio-economic responsibilities and attitudes about the post-retired life.

As already discussed (Fig. 5.6) that those drawing more than their last pay drawn at the time of retirement from Haryana were nearly 95 per cent of the total employed ex-servicemen from the State, whereas for Bihar, the figure of the same goes down to 60 per cent only. Similarly, the rate of those drawing less than their last pay drawn at the time of retirement is six times higher in Bihar than that of Haryana. One of the important reasons for the less salary earnings for those employed in Bihar is the fact that a great number of them do not find a place in Government jobs and, therefore, have to compromise with either working with private business houses or security agencies where salary offered to ex-servicemen is quite low. In Haryana nearly 75 per cent of the employed ex-servicemen found a place in various Government services, whereas the corresponding figure for the same in Bihar is only about 40 per cent (Fig. 6.2). Less representation in Government services in Bihar can be explained by the fact that there ex-servicemen are given no reservation in employment whereas, in Haryana, 17 per cent of the vacancies falling for classes III and IV posts are kept reserved for ex-servicemen (HLC: 1984, pp.153-54). In terms of employment opportunities, the ex-servicemen of Haryana are favourably placed because a number of them find Delhi as their major catchment area. Road conditions between Haryana and Delhi are very good, considering the overall road condition in India. Inhabitants of Gurgaon, Faridabad, Sonepat, Panipat, Rohtak, etc., can much more conveniently work in Delhi while living in their respective district. The Delhi Transport Corporation (DTC) is rife with the ex-MT drivers of the Indian Army and a good number of them are drawn from Haryana. There are a number of Public Sector Undertakings and Central Government Departments in Delhi which strictly follow the roaster system for filling up vacancies reserved for the ex-servicemen for Groups C and D posts. It is not expected that ex-servicemen from far-flung areas will be attracted for these posts. The reason why they want to stick to their native place has already been discussed. Therefore, most of the reserved vacancies arising in Delhi are filled with *Haryanvi* ex-servicemen. Consequently, ex-servicemen of Haryana, in terms of employment opportunities, are doubly benefited. First, reservation by the Government of Haryana is maximum compared to the rest of India (17% for Groups C and D posts), the implementation of which is strictly followed. Second, due to spatial proximity, vast employment opportunities arising in Delhi are tapped by the ex-servicemen of Haryana. They also participate in the Weekly Employment Market

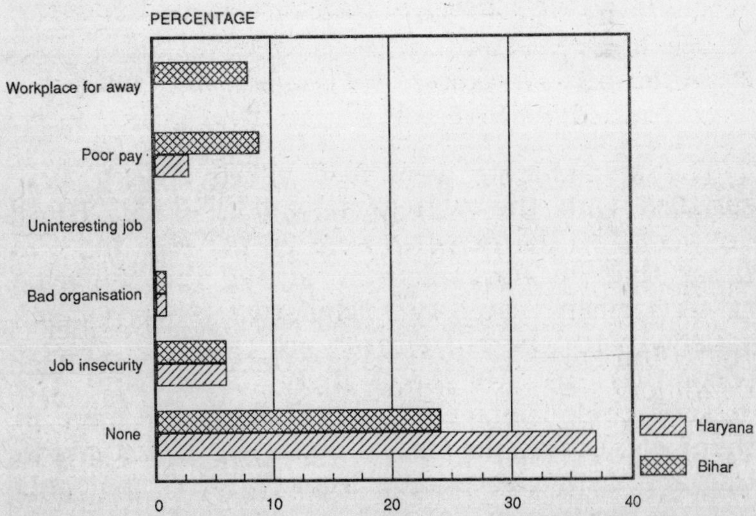

FIG. 6.12: Statewise Distribution of Ex-Servicemen's Rationale for Dislike of Job at Hand

organised by the Directorate of Re-settlement, New Delhi, and with their help they get quicker employment.

The fact that in Haryana employed ex-servicemen find better job conditions is verifiable from several other angles. In Haryana, those who do not give any reason for disliking their job form around 80 per cent of the employed ex-servicemen of the State whereas the corresponding figure for the same in Bihar is just 50 per cent (Fig. 6.12).

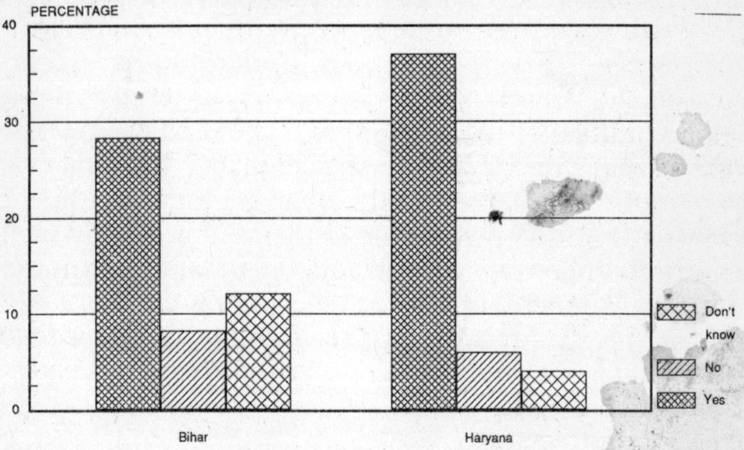

FIG. 6.13: **Ex-Servicemen's Self Reception about Satisfaction with Current Job**

The respondents were also asked if they were satisfied with the current jobs (Fig. 6.13). Those answering in the negative were 30 per cent more in Bihar than in Haryana from among the employed ex-servicemen category. Similarly, ex-servicemen satisfied with the current job are clearly in greater proportion in Haryana than in Bihar. The ex-servicemen ambivalent on the issue are more in Bihar confirming the fact of better job conditions in Haryana. It is also evident from Fig. 6.12 that only the ex-servicemen of Bihar attribute 'distance between place of work and home' as one of the reasons for dislike of job at hand. The ex-servicemen of Haryana do not provide this reason probably because in Haryana road conditions and transport facilities are better.

We get similar trend when we try to understand the quality of self-employment ventures being undertaken by the ex-servicemen of the two States. Figures 6.14(a) and 6.14(b) show that the number of self-employed wanting jobs in Bihar is higher by seven per cent than that of Haryana. Although the difference is not quite marked, ex-servicemen of this category from the two States seek self-employment for two different reasons. In Haryana, those who want suitable employment do so in order to supplement their income over and above agricultural income and the pension. But often, self-employed ex-servicemen from Bihar look for a job either to sustain themselves or to sustain their agriculture. Again, it is less likely that the ex-servicemen of Bihar of this particular category will get a desired job whereas possibility for the same is greater in Haryana because of vast employment opportunity of the State and also that of Delhi.

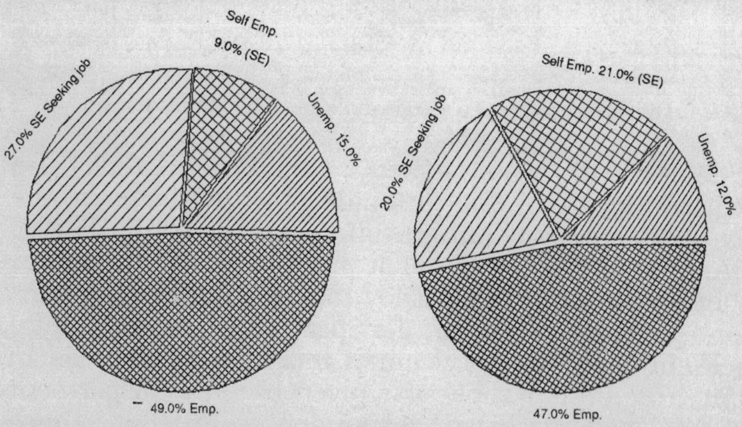

FIG. 6.14(a): Occupational Status of Ex-Servicemen: Bihar

FIG. 6.14(b): Occupational Status of Ex-Servicemen: Haryana

Only nine per cent of the total ex-servicemen interviewed in Bihar were fully self-employed whereas those reported as self-employed from Haryana were 21 per cent of the total sample for the State. This reveals that better agricultural productivity and market potentials of Haryana and its neighbouring regions provide better opportunities for profit-making through self-employment ventures. That is why those preferring self-employment as their second career instead of employment as second career are in greater percentage in Haryana than in Bihar.

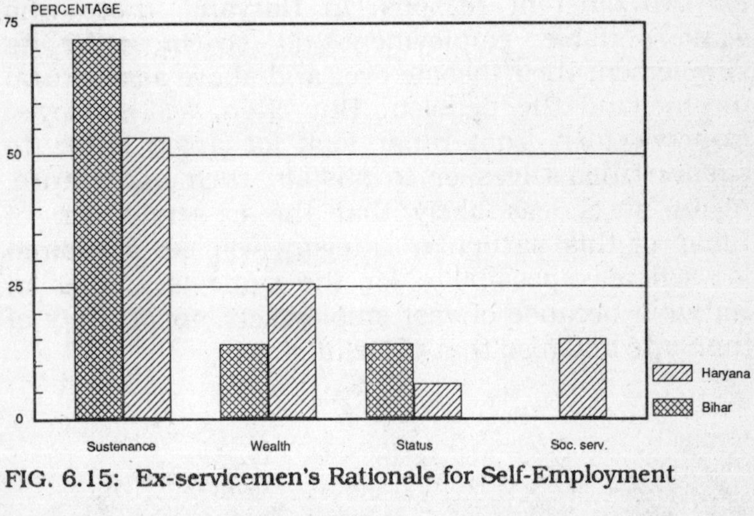

FIG. 6.15: Ex-servicemen's Rationale for Self-Employment

When it was asked why they took up self-employment, the rationale provided for it by the ex-Servicemen of Bihar differ greatly from that of Haryana which is explicit in Fig. 6.15. In Bihar, those who replied that they took up self-employment for sustenance were 72 per cent of the total self-employed ex-Servicemen interviewed whereas in Haryana similar reply was given by only 53 per cent of the self-employed respondents. Further, those who took up self-employment for wealth and status were equally distributed (14% each) and none opted for it due to 'service' from Bihar. In the case of Haryana, the corresponding figures were 26 per cent, 16 per cent and 15 per cent. Rationalisation given in favour of wealth, status or community service suggests the ambition of a man and his expectations from his self-employment venture. It is also revealed from the field data that the self-employed ex-servicemen of Haryana have better clarity about their self-employment ventures in terms of achieving monetary goals in the coming two years. The ex-servicemen of Haryana have also set higher material targets to be achieved in the next two years than those of Bihar as it is evident from Figs. 6.16(a) and 6.16(b).

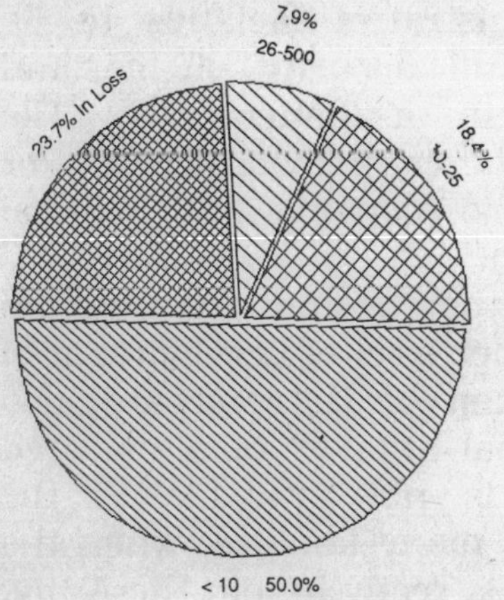

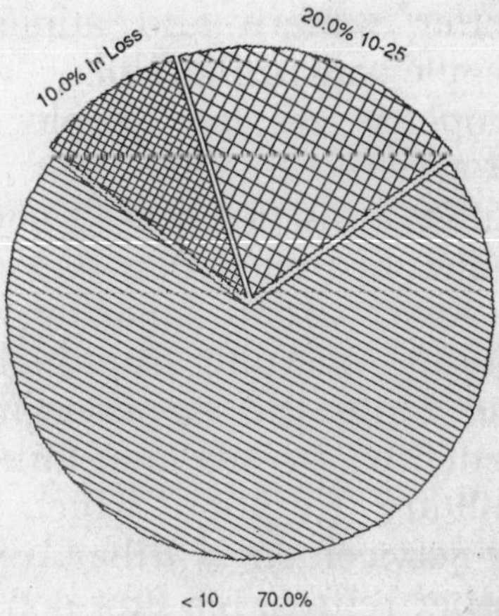

FIG. 6.16(a): Self-Employment Ex-Servicemen's Targeted Income in Next Two Years: Bihar (In Rs. Thousand)

FIG. 6.16(b): Self-Employment Ex-Servicemen's Targeted Income in Next Two Years: Haryana (In Rs. Thousand)

It is clear, therefore, that re-settlement in terms of re-employment and self-employment are better in Haryana than Bihar. But this is not all. The ex-servicemen living in Haryana get benefited in a number of other ways also which are not accessible to the ex-servicemen of Bihar. The overall development of Haryana has ensured better community living facilities for the people of its State. The better health, education and road conditions make the overall living comparatively safe and comfortable. In the hospitals or schools of Haryana comparatively there is lesser rush and quality of service is better and predictable than in Bihar. In Bihar, even for primary health care or education one must pay as the functioning of Government agencies even in such core sectors are corrupt and inefficient. In Haryana, comparatively there is better functioning of administration. Therefore basic amenities and services are provided free or on nominal cost and are assured. Further, being a smaller and socially homogeneous State, it provides better welfare and administrative facilities to its people ensuring safety and security of life and property of its people in a better way. The ex-servicemen, like any other person, benefit or suffer from the overall socio-economic and political milieu of a particular region.

Apart from enjoying the overall institutional support accruing from higher level of development of the State the ex-servicemen of Haryana are also benefited by the non-formal support of a matured military tradition which is not available to the ex-servicemen of Bihar. In many families, when the father retires, his first son is ready to join the Army. Even those who join Army for the first time from their family history do not find it difficult to find a *fauzi* among men of the paternal or maternal relatives. All these provide an environment, which makes the re-settlement of ex-servicemen of Haryana comfortable. In a way, joining the Army and returning home after retirement becomes a common feature of the community life of rural Haryana. A *fauzi* appears in almost all popular *Haryanvi* folk-song or dance-drama and, therefore, he is not a stranger in the community. Having been quickly absorbed in the village society, he is very much a part of it.

The folk culture of Haryana is full of songs, dance-drama with army and armymen as its central theme. These folk performances inspire its youth in a great way to join the Army, they eulogise the chivalrous and honour and sympathise with the bereaved. Pandit Deep Chand, one of the proponents of *Haryanvi* folk-stage, was conferred the title of "Rai Bahadur" for inspiring the *Haryanvi* youth to join the British Army during the First World War.[1] In between his every stage performance, irrespective of its theme, he would call upon the youth among the audience to join the Army. And finally at the end of the performance there would be a luring chorus:[2]

O ye get enlished, ye doorstep stand recruits

Here ye have rugged shoes there get new boot
Here ye have dirty rags there will get new suit
Here ye have dry breads there get biscuit
Here ye are despised there get salute

O ye get enlisted, ye doorstep stand recruits

The brave youngmen of Haryana fought with the Germans in the First World War on behalf of the British Army. According to a *Haryanvi* folk-song Platoon No. 6 of the British Indian Army comprising the *Haryanvi* youth suffered mass casualty in the battle. The song curses the Germans for the mass killings and also abuses the Britishers for air-lifting its youth to the battle-field. But it eulogises and sympathises with the youth of Platoon No. 6 which suffered mass casualty in the field.[3]

The military tradition of Haryana also gets manifested through numerous songs sung for the wife of a soldier.[4] Its theme invariably has a sympathetic view of the wife of a *fauzi*, depicting her woes and agonies particularly during the absence of her husband. Such songs are clear examples of spontaneous cultural (informal) support to the deprived persons in society. Although by singing or listening to such songs the wife of a serving *jawan* cannot bring her husband from the field posting, these do have a soothing effect and reduce the pains of abnormal estrangement. The ex-servicemen in Haryana, therefore, are not only part of the *Haryanvi* composite culture but they also add flavour to it. This is not so in the case of Bihar. Although people from Bihar and the Punjab began contributing their young men to Company's Army almost simultaneously, the recruitment from Bihar and Oudh was deliberately stopped after 1857 by the British Government. Therefore, the military tradition of Bihar got terminated. The *Bihari* recruits are now joining Army in greater number and a new military tradition is in the offing. The popular Bhojpuri skit of Rameshwar Singh Kashyap in the name and style of "*Loha Singh*" is a manifestation of this changing trend. But this is not enough to establish a tradition. It requires time for any tradition to get built up.

In the introductory chapter we have tried to explain how re-settlement works as a major social process in developing societies. There are many social categories other than the ex-servicemen which also fulfil the "conditions of re-settlement" and, therefore, become a subject-matter of re-settlement. Although the military tradition of Bihar is yet to mature, the tradition of emigration of labourers from Bihar, is fairly long. Since the migrant labourers of Bihar are also governed by the conditions of re-settlement it will not be inappropriate to see in brief how folk-culture has responded to this major social category (migrating labourers) of the region. One may find it interesting that the folk-culture of Bihar has responded as vigorously in the case of migrant labourers as it responded in the case of ex-Servicemen of Haryana.

A popular form of song and dance-drama called "*Bidesia*" grew out of recurrent emigration and immigration of the serving castes of Bihar and Eastern U.P. (particularly of the Bhojpuri belt) to Calçutta and other cities out of that linguistic belt, specially emigrating in eastward direction. Without going into the reason for what led to the recurrent migration[5] of such people which persists generation after generation, we are limiting our discussion here to explaining how folk culture of a particular region responds to the recurrent persistence of an activity and material needs associated with it. And, furthermore, how far such culture responses through its various mechanisms try to maintain equilibrium in absence of any formal institution coming up to take up the responsibility. Various songs and dance-dramas of a particular region and especially those under discussion intend to focus at mainly two themes – (a) the emigrated worker in the city suffering deprivations in various forms and (b) wife and children of the deprived worker staying back in the villages and suffering the kinds of difficulties which may normally arise in absence of a head of the household. The target audience of the village stage performances also includes those who have returned to the village after their work tenure in the cities among their friends and relatives and rural folk of the area in general. What is more important is the impact of the culture in the Bhojpuri belt of Bihar, its attraction and consequent mass participation. It conveys certain messages which are very familiar and easily understood by the people to whom it is shown. The songs and dance-drama of *Bidesia*, therefore, at once explains the historicity and recurrence of emigration and difficulties arising out of it for both the emigrating worker and his family members living behind in the village.

Bhikhari Thankur (1887-1971),[6] the proponent of the *Bidesia* form of stage narrating entire process of migration on stage, was himself a barber emigrated to Kharagpur (a suburban city of Calcutta) from Qutabpur, Saran (Bihar) for having better rewards for his traditional job. In the process, the gifted man innovated a form of stage entertainment for his fellow emigrants which was so profound that it quickly captured the minds of the rural folk of the entire Bhojpuri belts. The *Bidesia* show has four major parts: *Bidesi* (the emigrant), *Pyari Sundari* (wife of the emigrant), *Batohi* (the traveller) and *Rakhail* (the concubine). The plot of *Bidesia* revolves round its hero called *Bidesi* who emigrates to Calcutta driven by its charms and prospects to make money. In Calcutta he gets deviated . . . starts living with a concubine and becomes father of two sons from the relationship. The unbearable estrangements and difficulties of living alone in the in-laws' place prompts *Pyari* to urge *Batohi* (a traveller) to find out her husband in Calcutta and persuade him to come back to her soon. *Bidesi* gets persuaded by *Batohi* and returns home and meets his wife. Soon after, the concubine also reaches there with her two sons. The 'entire family' meets and with that the show ends. Most of the dialogues of the show have been delivered in numerous forms of Bhojpuri folk songs with musical instrument, chorus and ample mass participation.

Bidesi symbolises the fate of a common emigrant crushed between the responsibility of village (*Pyari*) and liability of the city (*Rakhail*). *Batohi* symbolises the cultural pull which persuades *Bidesi* to return home and saves him from getting lost to the city. *Bidesi*'s home does not only receive him but also accepts his liabilities – symbolised by the concubine and her two sons. The message is: one can get ultimate security and comfort only at one's home – and one's home, one's culture is ever ready to receive its members without looking into one's demerits so sternly.

It is clear, therefore, that the folk-culture of Bihar has responded favourably to its migrant labourers and its military tradition is yet to mature. The folk-culture of Bihar does not provide the kind of support being currently extended to by the ex-servicemen of Haryana. Due to the lack of a mature military tradition and lesser numerical strength an ex-serviceman in Bihar is easily spotted and therefore, he feels rather uncomfortable. Lack of tradition makes his re-settlement more difficult as his family members have not learnt to appreciate what a *fauzi* wants or expects when he returns home. In Haryana, re-settlement of ex-servicemen is a part of the collective process of society, whereas in Bihar, by and large, it remains an individual struggle.

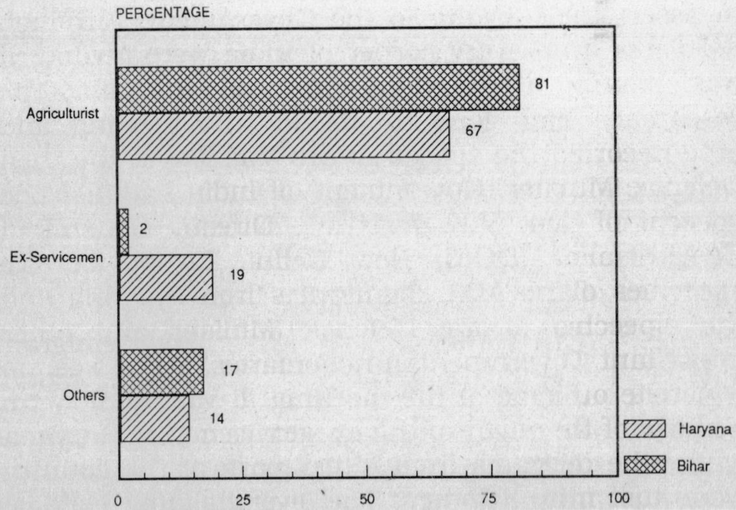

FIG. 6.17: Occupation of Ex-Servicemen's Fathers

The fact that Haryana has better military tradition is also evident from Fig. 6.17 wherein as many as 19 per cent of the ex-servicemen's fathers have been shown as having worked in the Indian Army whereas the figure for the same from Bihar is only two per cent.

The additional benefit that the ex-servicemen of Haryana enjoy is their numerical preponderance in the State which enables them to work as a politically effective group both in State politics as well as politics of All-India Ex-Services League (AIXL), New Delhi. While a number of ex-servicemen get elected to Haryana Legislative Assembly in every election and invariably they also find place in the State Cabinet, their numerical preponderance and spatial proximity with Delhi ensures them a very influential position in the affairs of AIXL, New Delhi. All key positions in the AIXL office get occupied by the ex-Servicemen of Haryana. All the rallies organised by the AIXL have a *Haryanvi* overtone. In 1986 an All-India Ex-Services rally was organised by the AIXL at the outskirts of Delhi to press their demands and to assert their loyalty to the Government. Although delegates from every corner of India were invited, it was mainly a *Haryanvi* show all through. The researcher had gone to attend this meeting and tape-recorded the speech of Sri V.P. Singh, the then Defence Minister, Government of India, and also the speech of Gen. V.K. Avasthy, Director General of Re-settlement (DGR), New Delhi. Except for the speeches of the AIXL dignitaries from Haryana and the speeches of the Defence Minister and other important Government functionaries, there was no concrete outcome of the meeting. It was, as it were, a show of the might of the ex-servicemen of Haryana while the delegates from other parts of the country were just mute listeners. The overwhelming political clout of the ex-servicemen of Haryana is also evident from our field data. The respondents were asked whether ex-servicemen could emerge as a political force in the country. Those who replied in the affirmative from Haryana were more than those so replying from Bihar (Fig. 6.18).

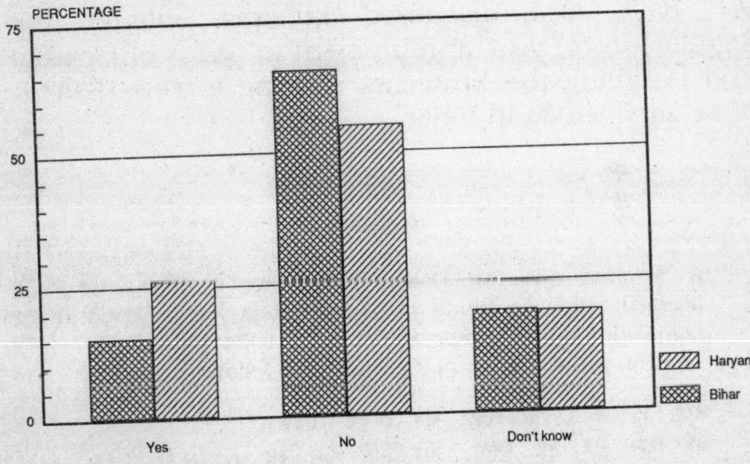

FIG. 6.18: Self-Perception of Ex-Servicemen as a Major Political Force.

Ultimately when we take into consideration the overall retired life ratings of the ex-servicemen of Bihar and Haryana, we find that those rating it as very good, better, good, worse and worst were 11, 15, 24, 30 and 19 per cent in Bihar and 5, 16, 31, 35 and 13 per cent in Haryana, respectively, of the total sample covered for each State. It is clear that the percentage of ex-servicemen having worst post-retired experiences in Haryana were less than in Bihar in nearly the same proportion as those experiencing it as very good were more in Bihar than in Haryana. The sharp fluctuation in the responses of Bihar towards the two extreme responses suggest that re-settlement of ex-servicemen in the State is not even. For proper understanding of such fluctuations, sociological explanations are required which are being attempted in the subsequent chapters. Thus, it is clear in the present chapter that regional differences affect to a large extent, the quality of re-settlement of ex-servicemen in India. We have also discussed in this chapter the significance of year of retirement in terms of locating and handling the problems relating to resettlement of ex-servicemen in India.

NOTES

1. A detailed note on Deep Chand Age in *Haryanvi* Folk literature can be found in Shastri Raja Ram, *Haryana Ka Lok Sahitya, Lok Sampark*, Haryana, 1984, pp.148-50.
2. The Haryanvi text of the Chorus is as follows:

   भरती हो ले रै, तेर बाहर खड़ै रंगरूट ॥टेक॥
   अड़े मिलै तन्ने टूटे लित्तर, ओडै मिलें फुल बूट । भरती हो ले रै ... ।
   अड़े मिलै तन्ने टूटे चिथड़ै, ओडै मिलेगें सूट । भरती हो ले रै ... ।
   अड़े मिलै तन्ने सूखे टिक्कड़, ओडै मिलेगें बिस्कूट । भरती हो ले रै ... ।
   अड़े मिलै तन्ने धक्का मूक्की, ओडै मिलेगें सेल्यूट । भरती हो ले रै ... ।

   See *ibid.*, p.150.
3. The Haryanvi text of the folk-song is as follows:

   तेरा जरमन जाईयो सत्यानास आज ना तड़क
   तन्ने मारे विराणे पूत झाझां मैं भर कै ।
   जरमन नै गोला मार्या, जा फूट्या अम्बर मैं
   गारद ते सिपाई भाज्जे, रोट्टी छोड़ गए लंगर मैं
   रै, उन बीरां का के जीना, जिनके बाल्लम छः नम्बर मैं ।

   See *ibid.*, p. 8.
4. The book published by the Director, *Lok Sampark*, Haryana, *ibid.*, has in its folk song part a separate section on "the Soldier wife" containing as many as 16 folk songs which depict different facets of a soldier's wife in Haryana.
5. The history of migration of Biharis to Calcutta is an old as the city itself. Although the rural push duc to devastating and recurrent famines acted as a major factor for perpetual

migration, the pull of Calcutta – its fancies and charms have always worked as an independent factor in emigrants' psyche. It is a pity that in the preparations of third centenary of the establishment of Calcutta, those who have continued to serve its middle classes and elite seem to be completely, forgotten.

6. Vidyarthi, Avinash Chandra (ed.), *Bhikhari Thakur Granthawali*, Part-I, Lok Kalakar Bhikhari Thakur Ashram, Qutabpur (Saran), Bihar, 1979. The work contains only the compilations, of Bhikhari Thakur's work in Bhojpuri, without any translation or commentary on it. This part includes, *Bidesia, Bhai Birodh, Beti Biyog, Kaliyug Prem* and *Radheshyam Bahar.*

7

FACTORS INFLUENCING RE-SETTLEMENT: Caste and Rank

IT HAS been noticed so far how temporal and spatial factors tend to affect the re-settlement process of the ex-servicemen in India. However, temporal (or historical) and spatial (or regional) approaches, though important, do not provide adequate explanation of a problem because most problems are socially determined by various social forces operating in a society. The ex-servicemen are also an integral part of our society. Their status in terms of particular caste or class plays a vital role in their re-settlement. A number of sociologists have demonstrated a definite nexus between caste and class in India which is popularly known as caste-class continuum in sociological phraseology. In the present section we intend to assess the comparative role of caste and class in the re-settlement of ex-Servicemen in India and at the end we will try to verify if the caste-class continuum in the case of re-settlement of ex-Servicemen exists or not.

Caste as a Factor Influencing Re-settlement of Ex-servicemen

It is found that in the Indian Army a particular caste from a particular region gets recruited in greater number than others from the same region. The *USI*

Journal of the late 19th century is replete with the articles and monographs on warrior castes, mostly written by the British officers of the Army of British India (See note 15 of Chapter 2). The Regimental Histories are as old as the British Indian Army. Much emphasis was laid on segregating soldiers on the basis of caste and usually a regiment was named after the dominant caste of the region. If the regiment was named after a region, it was implicit that it was dominated by one or two castes of that particular region.

Since Independence, it is being encouraged to accommodate recruits from different castes, religions and regions in a regiment irrespective of its nomenclature. Even so, things have not changed much and representation of a particular class of people from a particular region in a particular regimental army remains more less unaffected.

For the purpose of the present study, castes were classified into five, namely

(1) *Upper*, including Brahmans, Bhumihars and Rajputs;
(2) *Middle*, including Jat, Gujjar, Ahir, Kurmi and Koiri;
(3) *The Scheduled Tribes* (henceforth being referred to as ST);
(4) *The Scheduled Castes* (henceforth being referred to as SC); and
(5) *Others*.

It is evident from Figs. 7.1(a) and 7.1(b) that the upper and middle castes have found nearly even representation in Bihar whereas middle castes reported from Haryana are double the number of the upper castes in the State. There is no one having reported as ST in Haryana whereas in Bihar they comprised 43 per cent of the total respondents. An explanation for the high turn up of STs from Bihar is that one of the districts selected as sample from Bihar was Ranchi, having overwhelmingly high proportion of tribals. Further, the tribals of the district have long traditions of serving the lower ranks of the Army. The representation of SCs from Haryana is nearly three times more than that of Bihar. Not many variations are found in the representation of other castes in the sample from the two States.

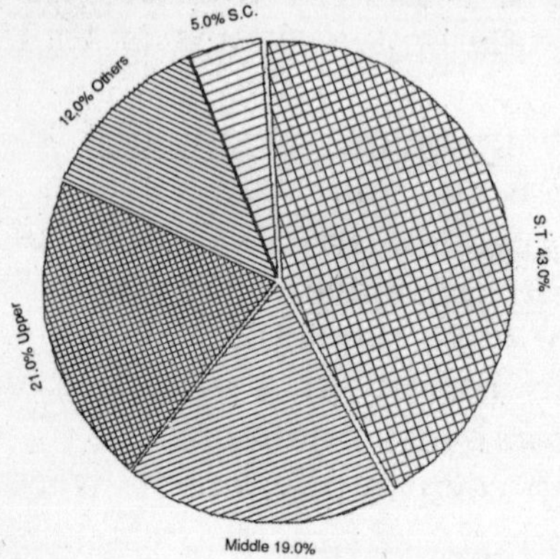

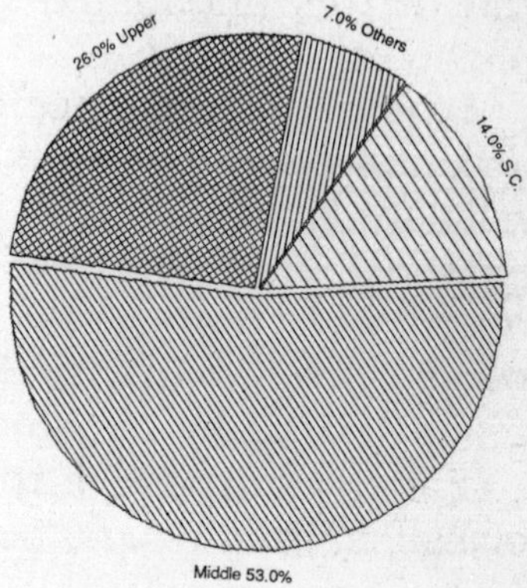

FIG. 7.1(a): Caste of Ex-Servicemen: Bihar

FIG. 7.1(b): Caste of Ex-Servicemen: Haryana

The data presented in Figs. 7.2(a) and 7.2(b) point out towards a clear correlation between caste and quality of re-settlement. In both the States those employed are more from the upper castes than any other castes, i.e. 71 per cent (Bihar) and 69 per cent (Haryana). The SCs and middle castes have almost equal position in the employed category, i.e., 60 per cent and 58 per cent each of the sample selected for Bihar. The STs of the employed category of Bihar are 40 per cent of their sample. Other castes have 25 per cent employed status in the sample selected for the category in Bihar and 43 per cent of the same in Haryana. Similarly, lower caste ex-servicemen are

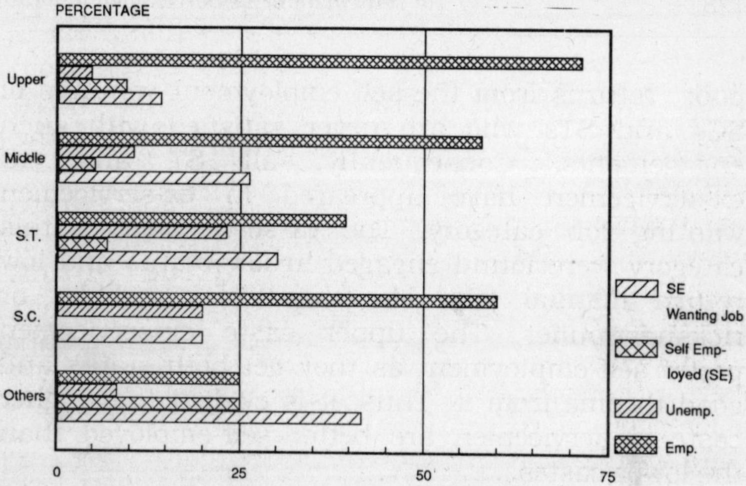

FIG. 7.2(a): Distribution of Ex-servicemen by Occupational Status and by Caste: Bihar

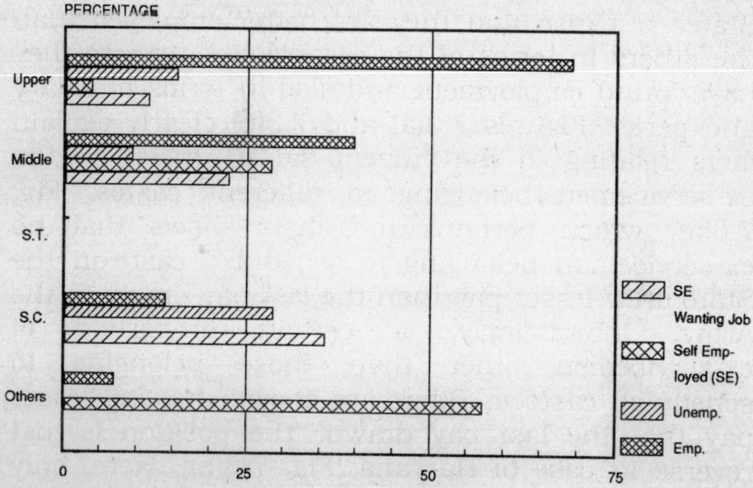

FIG. 7.2(b): Distribution of Ex-servicemen by Occupational Status and by Caste: Haryana

proportionately more unemployed than the higher cast ex-servicemen. It is interesting to note that no SC from both the States is self-employed. However, those from the "self-employed wanting job category", the Scheduled Castes of both Bihar and Haryana States have topped the rank in their respective columns in Figs. 7.2(a) and 7.2(b) This also shows poor returns from the self employment ventures of SCs and STs who are never satisfied with such engagements. Consequently, all ST and SC ex-servicemen have appreared in ex-servicemen wanting job category. The ex-servicemen of this category were found engaged in low status and low return manual jobs like those of a cobbler or rickshaw-puller. The upper caste ex-servicemen prefer self-employment as they get both status and good income from it. Thus, it is evident that higher caste ex-servicemen are better self-employed than the lower castes.

It is not only that the employed upper caste ex-servicemen are more in proportion in both the States but also that they are better employed than the others in terms of the organisations where they have found employment and also in terms of salary and perks. Figures 7.3(a) and 7.3(b) clearly explain facts relating to the current salary drawn by the ex-servicemen belonging to different castes. Fig. 7.3(a), which pertains to Bihar, shows that no ex-serviceman belonging to scheduled caste in the State drew lesser pay than the last pay drawn in the Army. Interestingly, a certain proportion of ex-servicemen other than those belonging to scheduled caste in Bihar are shown drawing lesser pay that the last pay drawn. The position is just reverse in case of Haryana [Fig. 7.3(b)]. Here, only the SC ex-servicemen are shown drawing lesser pay than the last pay drawn. Thus, a comparative analysis of the results of Figs. 7.3(a) and 7.3(b) do not indicate correlation between caste and amount of salary received. What is more clear from the analysis is the fact that the ex-servicemen of Haryana, by and large, are receiving better salary than Bihar, irrespective of the caste factor.

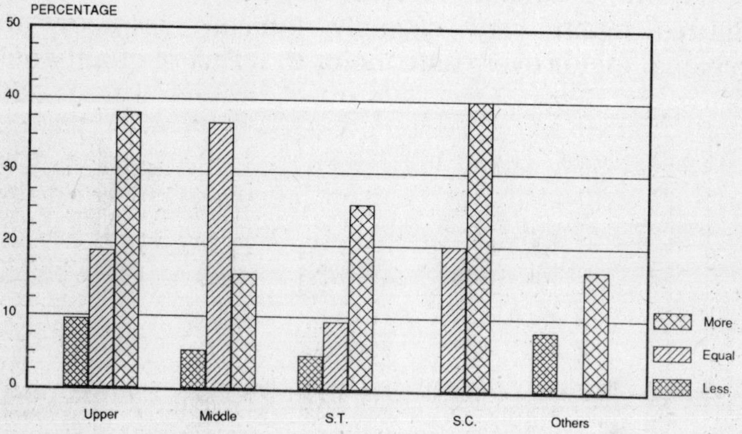

FIG. 7.3(a): Distribution of Ex-servicemen by Present Pay *vice* Last Pay Drawn and by Caste: Bihar

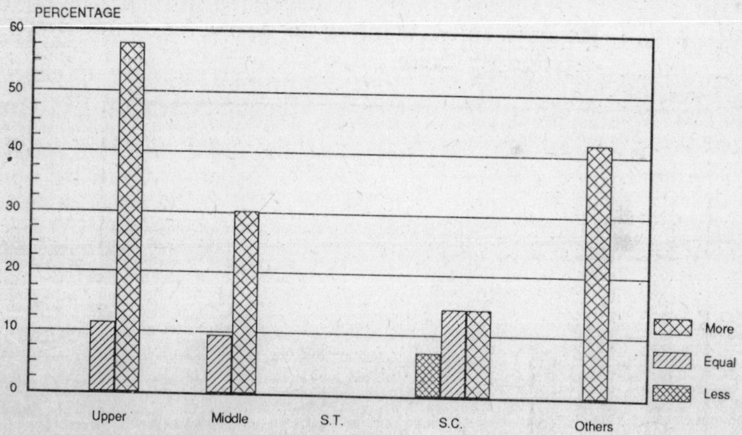

FIG. 7.3(b): Distribution of Ex-servicemen by Present Pay *vice* Last Pay Drawn and by Caste: Haryana

The upper caste ex-servicemen from both States have not been found satisfied with their jobs than the lower castes. When it was asked whether they applied for some better job, those replying in affirmative are mainly from upper castes, viz., 58 per cent from Bihar and 65 per cent from Haryana. A detailed position regarding this is contained in Figs.

7.4(a) and 7.4(b). A comparative analysis of the two figures again very strongly indicate primacy of regional factor over caste factor in terms of quality of

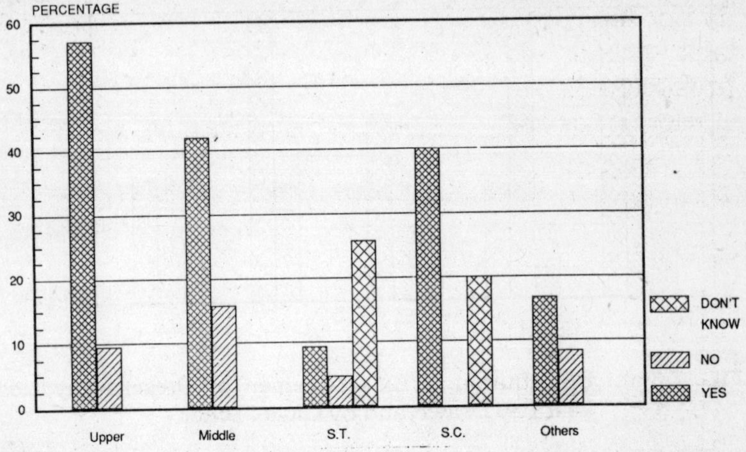

FIG. 7.4(a): Ex-servicemen Wanting to Apply for Some Better Job and By Caste: Bihar

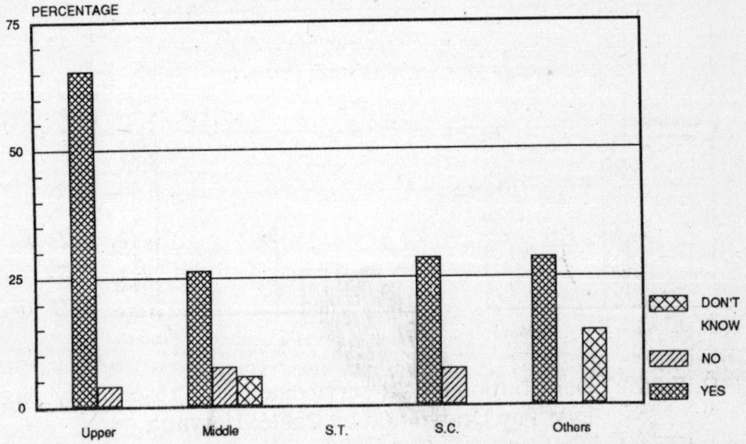

FIG. 7.4(b): Ex-servicemen Wanting to Apply for Some Better Job and By Caste: Haryana

resettlement. On the whole, those not wanting any change in job or indecisive on the matter are proportionately more is Bihar irrespective of the caste factor. However, impressive percentage of those replying 'Don't know' from ST and SC category of ex-servicemen in Bihar indicate that either they do not have knowledge about better openings or they lack proper motivation to try for a better job prospect.

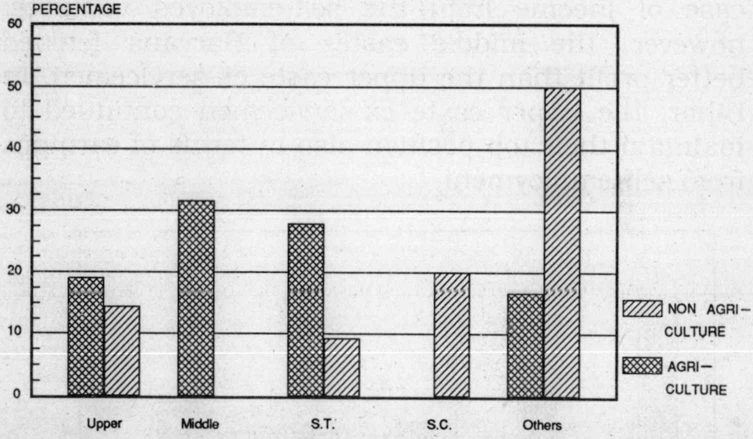

FIG. 7.5(a): Self-employed Ex-servicemen's Major Source of Income and by Caste: Bihar

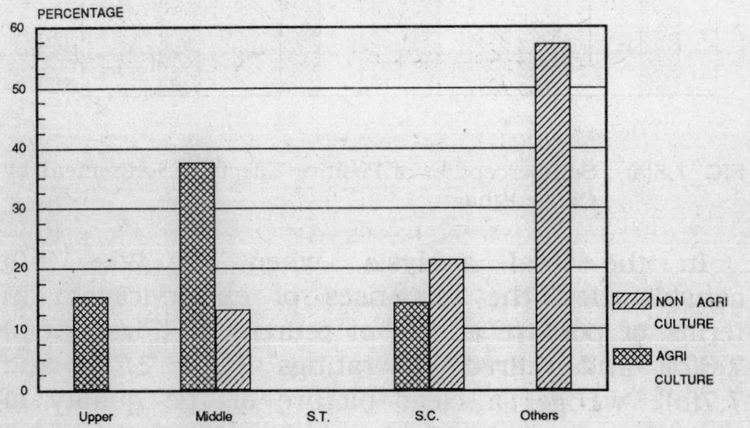

FIG. 7.5(b): Self-employed Ex-servicemen's Major Source of Income and by Caste: Haryana

In case of self-employment however, the caste factor has shown greater significance. Agriculture, by way of self-employment, has been mostly accepted by the middle castes. Figures 7.5(a) and 7.5(b) explain the point. All the SCs showing their self-employment under the category "non-agriculture" in Figs. 7.5(a) and 7.5(b) were engaged in their traditional service jobs after retirement. In case of income from the self-employed ventures, however, the middle castes of Haryana fetched better profit than the upper caste ex-servicemen. In Bihar, the upper caste ex-servicemen continued to maintain their top position also in terms of earnings from self-employment.

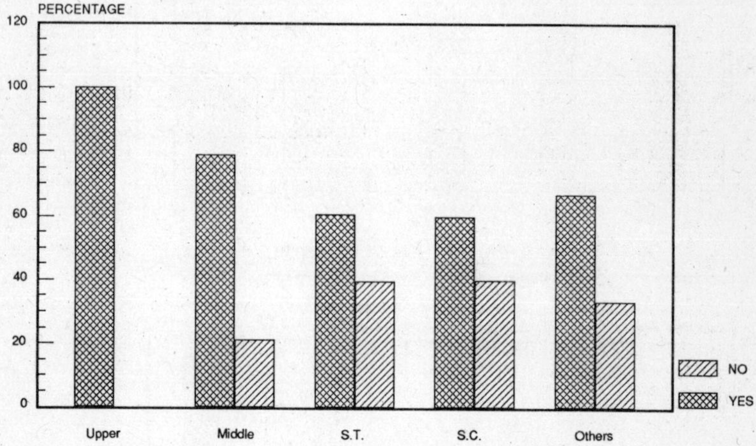

FIG. 7.6(a) **Self-perception of Positive Effects of Retirement by Caste: Bihar**

In the final analysis, when we take into consideration the responses of ex-servicemen in terms of positive effects of retirement [Figs. 7.6(a) 7.6(b)] and retired life ratings [Figs. 7.7(a) and 7.7(b)], we get a clear picture of the quality of re-settlement being enjoyed by different castes ex-servicemen in the two States. All the upper caste ex-servicemen from Bihar had positive effects of retirement. Those replying as "no" from the category middle caste, ST, SC and others in Bihar are 21 per cent, 40 per cent, 40 per cent, and 33 per cent, respectively. In Haryana, however, out of 53 middle caste

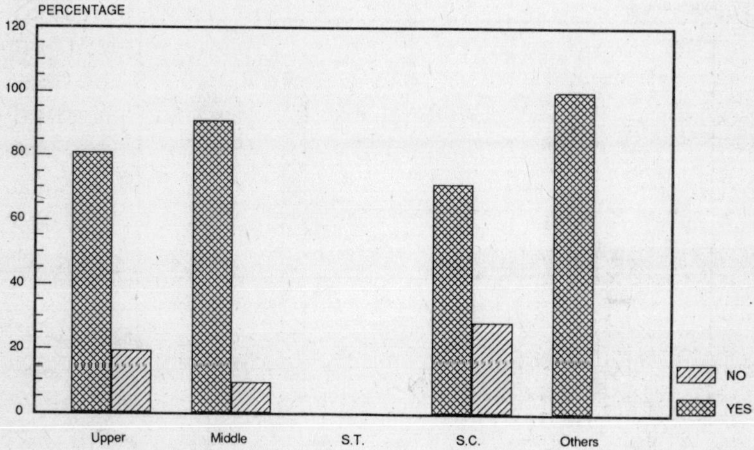

FIG. 7.6(b) Self-perception of Positive Effects of Retirement by Caste: Haryana

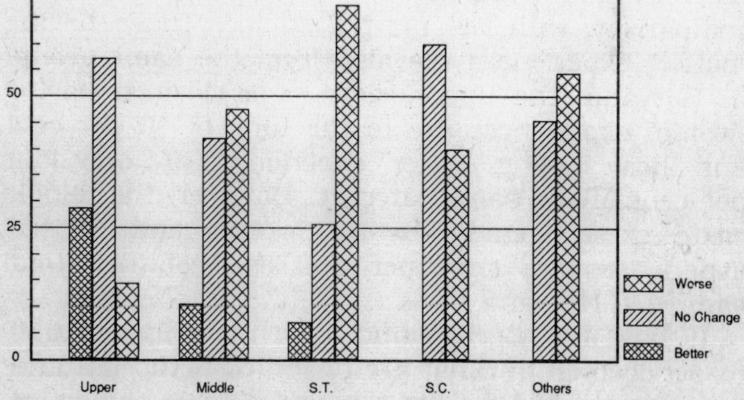

FIG. 7.7(a) Self-rating Retired *vice* Pre-retired Life: Bihar

ex-serviceman respondents only five (9%) have responded as "no" whereas out of 26 upper caste ex-Servicemen five (19%) responded as "no" while replying to the question on positive effects of retirement. Thus, the retired life ratings of the upper castes are better than those of the lower castes.

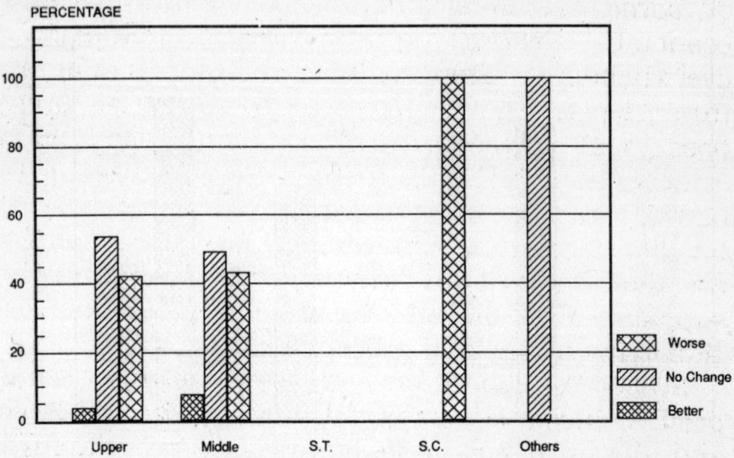

FIG. 7.7(b) Self-rating Retired *vice* Pre-retired Life: Haryana

Similarly, no upper caste ex-serviceman in Bihar had "worse" experience after retirement in comparison with his pre-retired life. Those having "better" experiences are also from the same group. In Haryana, the upper caste ex-servicemen having "worse" experiences are to the tune of 19 per cent and those having "better" experiences are only four per cent of the same category. However, the middle caste ex-servicemen having "worse" and "better" experiences are eight per cent each of their total sample in Haryana.

It has also been found that their upper caste ex-servicemen in Bihar are re-settled better than the samples studied for the remaining caste categories. But in Haryana the situation is somewhat different. Overall re-settlement of the middle caste ex-servicemen in Haryana is better than the upper castes. In a situation like this, the hypothesis, "higher the caste, better the quality of re-settlement" requires some further explanation for its verification or invalidation. If one views the middle castes of Haryana as 'dominant castes' the hypothesis stands verified. Whereas in Bihar, the upper castes in terms of *varna* hierarchy are also 'dominant' as their economic, political and numerical influence is overwhelming. The middle castes of Haryana through placed in the middle of the *varna* hierarchy, possess all the features of dominant castes.[1] It is evident, therefore, that there is no real discrepancy between castes status of the ex-servicemen and the quality of re-settlement when the understanding of the status of castes within *varna* framework are supplemented by additional concepts, such as 'dominant castes' and 'entrenched castes'.

No doubt, in terms of self-perception about positive effects of retirement [Figs. 7.6(a) and 7.6(b)] and also in terms of self rating *vice* pre-retired life [Figs. 7.7(a) and 7.7(b)] the upper caste ex-servicemen responses indicate relatively better resettlement. However, overall Statewise comparison do provide more positive responses from ex-servicemen belonging to Haryana than Bihar.

Rank as a Factor Influencing Re-settlement of Ex-servicemen

A general and brief reference of the class characteristics of ex-servicemen in India has already been made in Chapter 3. The 'Other Ranks' and 'Junior Commissionned Officers' of the Indian Army, by and large form a homogeneous class because the ex-servicemen of this class have identical social base and are usually recruited into army as sepoys. The usual entry points in the Indian Army are two-one as sepoys, meant for the ranks, and the other as 2nd Lieutenant, meant for the officers. Thus, two distinct classes in the army are inherent in its very recruitment process. Therefore, after retirement, invariably they retain the class in which they are initially recruited. We have already discussed why we have preferred to exclude the retired Commissioned Officers for the purpose of our present analysis.

Each of the two broader categories findings its basis in the two recruitment levels in the Indian Army, is separated by various ranks within the category. A sepoy at best expects to become Subedar Major although climbing up still further is not theoretically impossible. Similarly, a young officer recruit of the Indian Military Academy (IMA) can think of rising up to general's level while serving in the Army. Thus, the two broader classes of the Indian Army, by and large, remain each as mutually exclusive group with very small percentage of ORs and JCOs finding a place in the officer rank in their whole career.

The present work includes ex-Sepoys, ex-Nayaks, ex-Havaldars, ex-Naib Subedars, ex-Subedars and ex-Subedar Majors from Bihar and Haryana for the purpose of this analysis. In terms of the organisational hierarchy and rights and duties each rank is endowed with its special class attributes. However, in respect of pay and perks while in service and its consequent relationship with pension and relief after retirement, the six ranks mentioned in the study can be broadly divided into three. Thus, total maximum pay drawn by Sepoy Group C, Havaldar Group C and Subedar Group C in 1984 Rs.732, Rs.900 and Rs.1,365, respectively.[2] Similarly, in 1984 were the retirement benefits accruing to the said ranks were Rs.269, Rs.383 and Rs.773, respectively.[3] The ranks in terms of post-retirement pension and relief can be broadly viewed as two distinct analytical category to bring about meaningful comparison in our analysis and discussion. These are Sepoy and Havaldar ranks on the one hand (including Sepoy, L/NK, NK), and all the three grades of Subedar rank (including Naib Subedar, Subedar and Subedar Major) on the other. The two categories will be three-forths termed as OR and JCO ranks.

The rank of an ex-servicemen explains a number of important factors which may have direct bearing on his quality of re-settlement. Mere knowledge of the rank of an ex-serviceman roughly reveals at least three important factors having great relevance in his re-settlement:

(a) age at which he may have retired;
(b) the number of years of service he may have put in before retirement; and
(c) the amount of pension and relief being received by him every month.

As we shall find in our discussion, each of the three factors is positively correlated with rank, i.e., higher the rank greater the age of retirement, length of service and/or pension and relief or *vice versa*.

The correlation between rank and age of retirement is evident. Age of retirement affects the re-settlement of the ex-servicemen in two important ways:

(1) It determines to a large extent the responsibilities of an ex-serviceman, viz., size of family, number and age group of children, stage of their education, etc.
(2) It determines prospects of employability of an ex-serviceman for the civilian posts.

The age of initial recruitment into the army usually coincides with the age of marriage of the rank ex-servicemen. Incidentally, we may mention that for the officer ex-servicemen, marriage takes between four and eight years after getting commissioned in the Army and in a great many cases the time taken is even longer. Now returning to the rank ex-servicemen, it is common to find that they have their first child soon after their marriage. The generation which we interviewed, in our fieldwork, did not seem to have used any method for the delay of the birth of their first child though a great number of them subsequently accepted some family planning device either for the delay in or prevention of birth of the second or third child. Thus, generally speaking, when a sepoy comes out of the Army, his first child is roughly around 10 years old and in case of a Havaldar and Subedar, the age of the first child is 15 years and 20 years, respectively. In other words, when a sepoy returns home after retirement he finds his first child studying at the primary level. A Havaldar's first child is at secondary level. And a Subedar's first child is either employed in the Army or looking for a civilian job. The age and sex of the first child, especially in a lower middle class family, explains a lot deal about the kind and amount of pressure and responsibility an ex-serviceman father may be having.

The prospects of employment are also greater for the higher ranks than for the lower ranks. For the lower ranks, whereas their supply in the job market is abundant, demands are few. As already discussed, the general expectation is that an ex-serviceman is suitable for the job of Security Guard. But in almost all the para-military forces such as the Border Security Force (BSF), the Central Industrial Security Force (CISF) and the Railway Protection Force (RPF) etc., there is direct entry system at the sepoy level. Therefore, a vast number of ex-servicemen retiring as Sepoy, Lance Naik or Naik fail to find a place in those forces. This is because of the simple reason that these forces, too, are required to maintain youthful profile of their respective forces. The Public Sector Banks and other Public Sector Undertakings do employ the ex-sepoy, Lance Naik/Naik (LNK/NK) as security-guards at their respective establishments. Here there is great rush of the ex-sepoy LNK/NK to find a place among the seats reserved for them. Apart from these, other avenues of employment as Security Guards are the Private Sector Factories/Establishments or Security Agencies, where payments are generally low and irregular and the work conditions are infavourable.

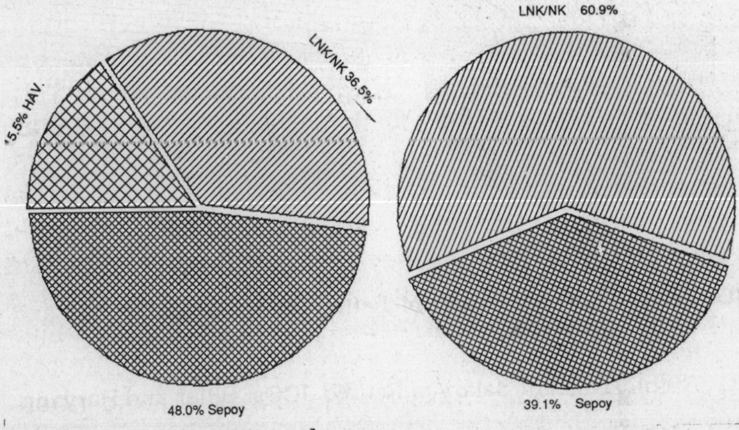

FIG. 7.8(a) Distribution of Unemployed Ex-servicemen: Bihar

FIG. 7.8 (b) Distribution of Unemployed Ex-servicemen: Haryana

The employability of ex-Havaldar and above ranks are much better both in the Public and Private sectors. First of all, the supply of those ranks in the job market is very limited because of the very restricted promotion system in the Army. Secondly, there is great demand for them in almost every force to take up supervisory position in the force for ensuring discipline and turn-out. The fact that the demand for employment of the ex-servicemen in job market increases with the increase in their ranks is also evident from Figs. 7.8(a) and 7.8(b). The figures show nil unemployment for JCO ranks. Only 15.5 per cent of ex-Havaldars in Bihar are unemployed. In Haryana, no ex-Havaldar interviewed was found unemployes. The ex-JCOs from both the states were found either employed or suitably self-employed.

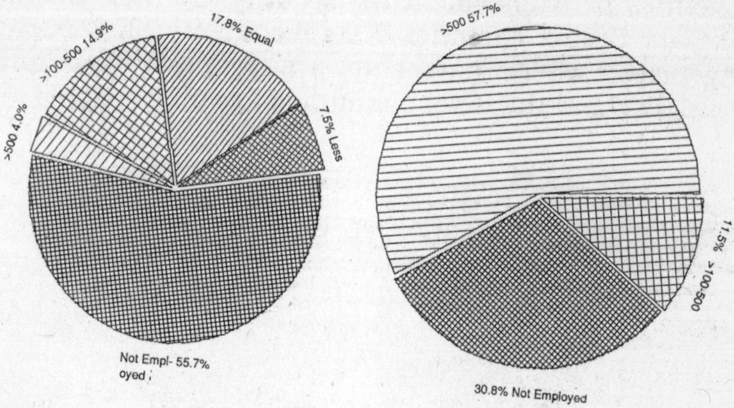

FIG. 7.9(a) Current Salary of Retired Other Ranks: Bihar and Haryana

FIG. 7.9(b) Current Salary of Retired JCOs: Bihar and Haryana

Various other indicators also strengthen the proof that the quality of re-settlement of high-ranking ex-servicemen is better than those occupying lower ranks. Figure 7.9(b) shows that the pay of all the employed ex-JCOs are either in the range of "more than Rs.100 but less than Rs.500" or "More than Rs.500 but less than Rs.1000". Those who accept less or equal pay than their last pay drawn are from the lower ranks [Fig. 7.9(a)]. However, it is clear to notice the regional factor operating hand in hand with the rank factor when the OR of Bihar drawing more than the last pay drawn are compared with those of Haryana. The analysis of data suggest that whereas only 12 per cent of the employed ex-sepoys from Bihar are getting more than last pay drawn, in the case of Haryana those having drawn the same are roughly double in terms of percentage.

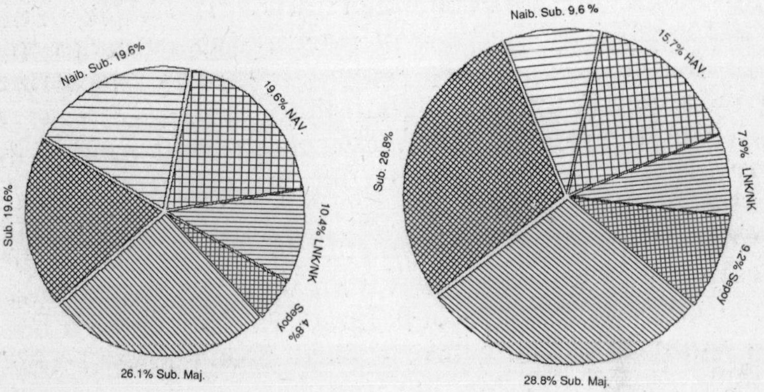

FIG. 7.10(a) Ex-servicemen Satisfied with the Current Job: Bihar

FIG. 7.10(b) Ex-servicemen Satisfied with the Current Job: Haryana

The rank-wise analysis of the employed ex-servicemen in relation to satisfaction with their respective jobs also reiterates the undisputable correlation between rank and the quality of re-settlement. Figures 7.10(a) and 7.10(b) show that on the whole, employed ex-servicemen have expressed their satisfaction with the job that they occupy. Those confirming their satisfaction with the job are much more than those disapproving or being undecided on the point. Around 65 per cent of the total employed ex-servicemen from Bihar and 85 per cent from Haryana expressed that they were satisfied with their post-retirement jobs. However, those replying in the negative or answering as undecided were more among the lower ranks. For example, in Bihar, the employed sepoys answering in the affirmative and negative were 30 per cent each of their total sample whereas 40 per cent were undecided on the matter. The negative response gradually decreases with the increase in the rank with negligible variation. The negative and undecided replies attain zero level in case of Subedar and Subedar Major ranks. The same trend is repeated in the case of Haryana also though the proportion of those replying in the negative/ undecided is much less than that of Bihar.

The self-employed ex-servicemen were probed in regard to "income targeted for the next two years". The higher ranks have set higher income targets from their self-employment ventures. The OR category of ex-servicemen from both the States have not only set lower income targets for themselves but a number of them have replied "Don't know". This reply is crucial for the purpose of our analysis because seldom correct estimates about income accruing or projected are provided by the respondents. Estimated income is one of the basic goals of any self-employment venture. If one is not certain about one's expected income it is unlikely that he will succeeded in his venture. The lack of clarity of goal explains, among many other things, the lack of training or exposure to the business being undertaken, lack of structural facilities and lack of interests, etc., all of which are essential requirements of success in any self-employment venture. It is interesting to note that those replying 'Don't know' have no representation in the last three columns meant for the ranks of Subedar level. Therefore, in terms of self-employment also, the re-settlement of higher rank ex-servicemen is better than the lower ranks.

A question was designed to assess the retired life ratings of all the categories of ex-servicemen *vice* their pre-retired life. This is an important dimension for assessing the quality of re-settlement of ex-servicemen. In a sense the question was applicable to all respondents, irrespective of their occupational status, year of retirement, etc. It was expected that all the respondents will choose one of the five options given in the question. However, out of the total sample of 200, only one respondent from Bihar declined to give any answer to the question. The analysis of data clearly affirm the point, higher the rank better the re-settlement.

All the Subedar Majors from both the States have responded as "very good", the highest rating in this five-point scale. Apart from the fact that all of them are meaningfully re-employed/self-employed, the additional factor contributing to this kind of response is the fact that attaining the rank of Subedar Major is the highest professional accomplishment in their service career. The rank Subedar Major is of great ornamental value even today. Therefore, if an ex-serviceman, fully contented with his pre-retired career achievement, gets red carpet welcome for the post-retired life also, he possibly cannot rate his career as less than the best. Those having "very good" experience from Sepoy to Havaldar levels are less than 10 per cent of their respective samples in both the States. On the contrary, the last three columns meant for officers of Subedar level show zero representation against the column meant for "worst" experiences. The "worst" retired life ratings gradually decreases with the increase in rank whereas best ("very good") retired life ratings increase with the increase in ranks.

The rank-wise discussion of the re-settlement of ex-servicemen, therefore, leads us to a proportion like this :

> The demand curve for the lowest rank in terms of rising family responsibilities is at its maximum whereas supply curve in terms of pension and second career prospects is at its minimum. With the increase in rank, whereas the demand curve goes down, the supply curve moves up. Hence, rank emerges as a crucial factor in determining

the quality of re-settlement of ex-servicemen in India.

So far two sociological factors, namely, caste and rank, influencing re-settlement patterns of ex-servicemen have been dealt with one by one. The discussion on each factor has confirmed the point that higher (ascribed or achieved) status positively contributes to the re-settlement of the ex-servicemen in India. If the proposition 'higher the caste, better the quality of re-settlement' is supplemented by another proposition 'higher the rank, better the quality of re-settlement', then it is pertinent to ask whether some or the other correlation exists between castes and rank as well. The analysis of data suggests that there exists a positive correlation between castes and rank. The higher castes ex-servicemen usually occupied higher ranks in the Army. The lower castes, specially the scheduled castes and the 'other castes' could seldom move beyond the rank of Havaldar. The respectable representation of scheduled tribes in the rank of Subedar, however, needs some clarification. All such ex-servicemen are Christians (STs) belonging to Ranchi district. Due to the impact of the role of Christian missionary activities, the Christian tribes of the Ranchi district are better placed than the Hindu tribes there. The level of education, income and health is comparatively very low among the Hindu Adivasis. Two Hindu Adivasi ex-servicemen were found pulling rickshaw in Ranchi town. Interestingly, the rickshaws which they pulled are owned by one of the their colleagues in the Army. The owner of the rickshaw *Khatal* is an ex-serviceman (Bengali-Kayastha by castes), having a decent house at the outstrikes of Ranchi. The non-Christian Adivasis invariably drank *'Hadia'*, (an indigenous beverage) and were quite ignorant about the re-settlement facilities being offered by the

Government. Most of the Christian ex-servicemen were tee-totallers, but having adequate knowledge about the post-retirement career prospects.

The fact which emerges from the discussion is that knowledge about the year of retirement of an ex-serviceman provides important insights in terms of locating the nature, form and magnitude of his resettlement problems. Currently retired ex-servicemen have much greater problems of resettlement than ex-servicemen retired say about five/six years ago. It has also been amply discussed as to how regional factors facilitate or hinder the process of resettlement of ex-servicemen in India. While discussing the relative influence of caste factor, we have noticed how regional factors have played more significant influence in the quality of resettlement. Yet, one cannot completely ignore caste as a factor influencing resettlement. Rank of ex-servicemen, as discussed, determine very strongly the prospects and quality of resettlement.

All the four factors discussed (two in the preceding chapter namely, time and region and two in the present chapter namely, caste and rank) have appeared to exercise their relative influences on the re-settlement patterns of ex-servicemen in India. In the absence of a sensitivity test, it is difficult to order their precise role in the re-settlement process. On the basis of feedback of qualitative data gathered from the field, however, we find may state that it is the rank which plays the more significant role among the four factors discussed.

NOTES

1. M.N. Srinivas "The Dominant Castes in Rampura", *American Anthropologists*, February, 1959.
2. *Report of the High Level Committee on Problems of Ex-Servicemen*, Govt. of India, p.138.
3. *Ibid.*, p.139.

8

PROSPECTS

IT HAS been noticed in the foregoing chapter that the ex-servicemen with higher ranks have a better chance of re-settlement than those occupying lower ranks. To recapitulate the point in brief, we have found the supply curve in terms of pension second-career opportunities and consequent financial returns gradually rising with the higher ranks whereas demand curve, in terms of ex-servicemen's responsibilities towards wife, children and near relatives, has witnessed a downward trend. Thus, higher rank ex-servicemen are doubly benefited; they get better second career returns against waning responsibilities whereas the lower ranks find zero or poorer returns against rising responsibilities. Besides, we have also seen factors such as year of retirement and State (region) providing greater insight into the problem when qualitative evaluation of re-settlement of ex-servicemen retiring in a given period from two unequally developed States (regions) are undertaken.

One can broadly discuss the prospects relating to the re-settlement of ex-servicemen in India in two ways. The discussion of first type emerges out of an enquiry which is essentially diagnostic.[1] The questions put are: What is the nature, form and extent of the malaise? How far is it similar to or different from other related problems? While discussing the enquiry of the second type an attempt will be made to understand the academic prospects of the enquiry of this type. Thus, the questions emerging from the diagnostic enquiry into the problem are: What is the sociological significance of the problem being discussed? Can the problems of ex-servicemen be viewed along with the problems of several other related social categories? Should the categories that are governed by the conditions of resettlement be studied in discrete manner or can we attain better understanding into the problems, once they are studied in an integrated fashion? In other words, is there a prospect or, more appropriately, an academic purpose in studying the re-settlement problems in our society under a new title, called *Sociology of Re-settlement*?

The second type of analysis is the discussion of the problem or the issue *per se* from the management viewpoint. The enquiry is essentially prognostic and the useful questions asked in this kind of inquiry are: What colour the issue will take if it is just ignored for a few years? What tangible benefits can be achieved if such and such resources are invested in tackling a specific problem? and so on.

Let us now explore the prospects of the problem already discussed both from diagnostic and prognostic viewpoints one by one.

The Prospects of Diagnostic Analysis

In the present study, we have tried to probe into the nature of the problems the ex-servicemen face and re-settlement as a method for resolving the same. To make an appraisal of the re-settlement process we have also tried to analyse the factors influencing re-settlement. While discussing the conditions governing re-settlement, we have found that there are several other social categories having similar conditions which govern the ex-servicemen. Therefore, a comparative analysis of two or more occupational categories governed by the conditions of re-settlement can be more insightful. Similarly, comparative study of different regions can also throw new lights into this area of research.

Similarly, the study of cultural responses to the process of re-settlement can be equally enriching. We have made quick references of longer military traditions of the *Haryanvis* in comparison to the Biharis. The longer military tradition of Haryana has reflected itself into folk-songs, stories and dramas. Although the cultural factors work in a very subtle manner, they carry profound impact on the overall re-settlement of ex-servicemen. They create culturally favourable environment for them. Therefore, in a familiar and favourable environment, even if an ex-serviceman has to wait for some time in taking up a suitable second career, he does not find himself out of place. Thus, the strains of unemployment are minimised and he feels more secure than his counterparts living in an environment either hostile or indifferent to their problems.

The Prospects of Prognostic Analysis[2]

While considering the prospects of the problem from the viewpoint of social engineering or manpower planning, one has to seek answers to some of the questions in the beginning. These are: Is the problem worth paying attention to at all? If so, to what extent? Further, when it comes to the question of actual formulation of action plan, the question asked is: How to provide, within all constraints, speedier re-settlement to the ex-Servicemen of the Junior Commissioned Officers and Other Ranks, particularly of underdeveloped regions?

Operationally, it means an exercise by the leaders and managers of the State to place the problem in the agenda of their action plan. Prioritisation of problems in the action plan of the managers of the system is usually done after considering what negative consequences the neglect of a problem can bring about rather than counting the benefits accruing once the problem is managed. While justifying the problem and stating various approaches to re-settlement, we have precisely discussed the pros and cons of giving immediate attention to the problem or hazards involved in ignoring it. It is pertinent to recapitulate here some of the main arguments already advanced with a few additional remarks.

It has been said that agriculture is no longer a viable full-time vocation for the majority of ex-servicemen, nor is the pension amount sufficient to meet the rising demands of the family. Therefore, a viable alternative for post-retirement vocation for them must be explored. Self-employment as an alternative is limited to agriculture and allied activities and in some cases transport and agencies run with the support of the Government. The study reveals that, for several reasons, it is hard to make an entrepreneur out of an ex-serviceman at least from the JCO or OR category. Thus, from the management viewpoint, their re-settlement implies a quick re-employment ensuring a salary at least equivalent to the last pay drawn in the Army so that they do not experience erosion of status. Consequently, as a strategy for ensuring quick re-settlement to the vulnerable and most populous (Other Rank) ex-servicemen, their automatic re-employment in various Government agencies in the vicinity of their native place should top the priority list of any strategy formulated for the re-settlement of ex-servicemen in India.

Although the lower ranks have shown the least sensitivity towards politics, they are the most dissatisfied group among the ex-servicemen. Most logical implication of the trend is that the dissatisfied low ranking and politically sensitive ex-servicemen of a particular region may be instigated to play a vanguard role in any (just or unjust) radical movement. This probability to join such a movement is strengthened by a variety of reasons: dissatisfaction with their existential conditions, arms training idleness and a state of perpetual unemployment particularly after around 15 years of tight Army schedule. Although it is a matter of independent research, the general impression one gets through media reports of the involvement of ex-servicemen in mobilisation and violence of Punjab and Gorkhaland problems cannot be entirely baseless. The large scale dissatisfaction among the ex-servicemen of Ranchi district and the indifference of the Zila Sainik Board and other responsible Government machineries in amelioration of their problems may be encashed by the leadership of Jharkhand movement in winning their whole-hearted active support. Although we have done a modest study under several constraints, we find ourselves under obligation to caution that if the ex-servicemen of Ranchi district are not re-settled properly, in immediate future, their problems may find an easy expression through the Jharkhand or such movement which has been gaining momentum in the region for quite some time.

Nevertheless, a rather positive reason for the immediate attention to their problems lies in the fact that every individual ex-serviceman of lower rank finds a sudden void in his life which persists so long as he is not suitably re-employed during his active life. A well thought out strategy for their lateral placement in different Government organisations will not only free the ex-servicemen from the void that they invariably face, but also that an optimum utilisation of time and money spent on their training can be taken care of.

Towards a Theoretical Framework

In the re-settlement process, we have found that the ex-servicemen enjoy both formal and non-formal support. For example, the Directorate of Re-settlement, Rajya and Zila Sainik Boards, All-India Ex-Services League, etc., are the institutions which exist in society to look after the re-settlement and welfare needs of the ex-servicemen. We have seen in Chapter 2 that the armymen have enjoyed non-formal support in society since time immemorial. As a professional category, they have always been treated as most privileged in society. The non-formal support in terms of appreciation, praise, reverence and preference in receiving small socio-economic privileges have been always reflected through the institutions, such as family, peer groups, villages, caste, tribe and region. This non-formal support gets accentuated and most generalised in times of war in the form of sympathetic public opinion of the entire Nation-State towards its defence personnel. During war, serving and retired services people are revered alike, in fact they become charismatic objects. What ex-servicemen have complained as the erosion of their *izzat* in recent time is essentially the comparison of a peace time public attitude towards them as against the mass euphoria of war-time. No society can afford to disrespect its defence personnel. They are the ultimate sanction of the State. Ex-servicemen, therefore, enjoy both formal and non-formal support in society in their re-settlement process. Apart from family, peer group, village, caste and tribe, even the cultural elements of a particular region, such as folk song, dance and drama, work in close harmony with non-formal institutions to emotionally "re-settle" the ex-servicemen returning home on retirement.[3]

The Three Ideal Types

It is clear, therefore, that the victims of re-settlement can get both formal and non-formal support in the re-settlement process. We have also seen in Chapter 1 that the ex-servicemen are not the only social category who are governed by the "conditions of re-settlement". Thus, based on the nature of re-settlement support and conditions of re-settlement we can arrive at a typology of re-settlement, which is given in Table 8.1.

TABLE 8.1: A Typology of Re-settlement

Typology	Re-settlement Support		Social category requiring resettlement
	Formal	Non-Formal	
EBR	+	+	Ex-Servicemen
NFR	-	+	Migrant Labourers
FR	+	-	Wholetimers of a cadre-based Party Persons displaced by the State for carrying out its development projects (e.g. displacements for making contonments, dams, industrial towonships, etc.) Refugees

EBR = Evenly Balanced Resettlement
NFR = Non-Formal Resettlement
FR = Formal Resettlement

The NFR Model

It has been discussed above and in the preceding chapters how ex-servicemen as a social category are governed by the conditions of re-settlement and how they get both formal and non-formal support in the re-settlement process. Thus, evenly balanced re-settlement, typology applicable to the ex-Servicemen is the one in which both formal and non-formal support are available in the re-settlement process.

In the NFR model of re-settlement whereas the non-formal support is available to the concerned group, formal support is unavailable. This is largely because the concerned parties of re-settlement of this type do not earn their livelihood under any formal institutional arrangement. They are the daily wage earning migrant labourers in the cities, selling their labour as and when there is demand for the same. They are not employed in strict sense of the term. They are either the artisan migrants selling their traditional skills in the cities on individual basis or selling their labour as menials, household servants, rickshaw-pullers or the contract workers in the low paid urban trade and industry. Examples of the first type are the *Chamars* (coblers), the *Dhobis* (washermen), the *Nais* (barbers), the *Kumhars* (potters), etc. The examples of the latter type are rickshaw-pullers, newspaper vendors, fruit and vegetable sellers, coolies and construction workers, etc. The latter type, therefore, engages itself in the non-traditional profession in the cities.

The daily wage earners, as stated above, have low and precarious income. They invariably live in inhuman and unhealthy conditions of the city slums. Majority of them return home in their middle age because by then they are physically exhausted which make them unfit for physical toil in the cities.

Since they are no longer productive they cannot sustain themselves in the cities. Therefore, they must go back to their village home for rest and care, preferably after planting their growing unemployed son(s) in the city.

In the NFR model, the jerk of deprivation is to be borne solely by the members of the primary group to which an individual belongs. In the EBR model, the depriving institution (for example, the State in case of ex-Servicemen) takes up the formal responsibility of the deprivations suffered in course of employment and thus formally lends its support in the re-settlement process, wherever necessary. In NFR model, on the contrary, those who deprive disappear from the scene - but for whom the deprivations were suffered still exist and are inexplicitly liable to lend the re-settlement support. A tacit understanding develops between those undertaking deprivation and for whom deprivation is undertaken to the effect that the latter will take care of the former when he returns to his village home fully exhausted in his middle age, both physically and emotionally.

The non-formal support of the NFR model also gets expression in folk songs, dance, drama, etc. The problems faced by the migrating labourers of the Bhojpuri belt of North India was beautifully captured by Bhikhari Thakur, a gifted Bhojpuri poet and talented artist, as noted earlier.

The work of Bhikhari Thakur is a representative pattern of numerous popular folk-traditions which manifestly entertain its clients and particularly satisfies all those who suffer deprivations of common nature in the process of their emigration and stay in the cities, and plan or expect re-settlement in their respective villages. Cultural responses to the process of re-settlement emerge out of the inevitability of the city migrants to come back to their home villages. The time when a migrant decides to re-settle in his village is the culmination point of his socio-psychological estrangement as well as physical incapacity to work in the city any further.

The FR Model

In the FR model it is evident that the formal support is available but non-formal support is lacking. The FR model includes all re-settlement processes where the deprived persons or their representatives directly seek compensation from the depriving institutions. The non-formal support of the family, etc., is not available as the victims of the FR model join the (depriving) institutions of their choice with altruistic motives. For example, if a young boy or girl becomes hardcore party member/whole-timer of a party contemplating radical changes in the system, he/she usually does so only after revolting or disappointing his/her parents. Since victims of the FR model do not identify themselves with their orientation home, the latter is not under obligation to support such persons in their re-settlement process. They usually expect support from the institutions they served and also get it.

For example, the hardcore and dedicated rank and file of any organised political party are the youth in their teens and twenties. Only few remain as wholetime party workers for their life time. Most of them after putting in five to ten years of their youth get dissatisfied and disillusioned because upward mobility in any political party is extremely difficult at least for the ranks. Consequently they want to settle down in their life; they want to live in a family and aspire for a regular source of livelihood. The depriving institutions do take care. The fellow party workers and comrades co-operate among themselves so that a hitherto dedicated worker leads a satisfied life outside and remains useful and faithful to his party throughout his life.

The re-settlement process of the whole-timers in

the Rashtriya Swayamsevak Sangh (RSS) may provide an interesting example of the 'Formal Resettlement' (FR). To become a *Pracharak* (wholetime propagator) in the RSS, a faithful *Swayamsevak* (volunteer) must be a man of high moral character usually having done second year of Officers Training Camp (popularly known as OTC). He can remain *Pracharak* as long as he is faithful to the *Sangh* and maintains his goodwill equally among the rank and file and the leadership. Some of the *Pracharaks* want to continue in the organisational status hierarchy of the RSS for the whole life. But quite a few want to lead a settled life outside the organisation fold to attend to their non-altruistic desires. Those wanting to lead a life outside RSS organisational heirarchy after relinquishing the status of *Pracharak*, find themselves in a very difficult situation. They must get some support for their socio-economic re-settlement. Although the RSS does not formally take up the responsibility of its ex-*Pracharaks*' re-settlement, usually he gets support from the *Swayamsevaks* of the *Sangh* rather than his ex-*non-formal* associations.

Reference Groups of the Ex-servicemen

Through a typology of re-settlement one can grasp the kind of re-settlement processes operating in society. Consequently, one can make a comparative judgement of the quality of re-settlement of a particular category in terms of others living in analogous conditions. But operationally, a subject of resettlement confronts and compares himself with persons of different social groups in his re-settlement process. They are the reference groups of the social category to which he belongs. Reference groups determine the psychological state of an individual and the potential collective action of the group with which he identifies himself. Although it was not intended to focus upon the reference groups of the ex-servicemen and their responses towards each of such groups, in course of our field-work and research such groups have spontaneously surfaced. We find it pertinent to make a note of these points.

It has been observed that an ex-serviceman is confronted with essentially three types of reference group:

(i) the young job seekers intending to get the job which the ex-serviceman aspires,
(ii) old friends of his age group who took up civilian employment near about the time when he joined the army and finally
(iii) old retired civilians leading relatively peaceful life after fulfilling most of their responsibilities as against the hard and difficult cases of old ex-servicemen still finding difficulties in fulfilling their responsibilities.

An attempt has been made in Table 8.2 to suitably present the three reference groups of ex-servicemen.

TABLE 8.2 Reference Groups of Ex-Servicemen and Types of (Negative) Responses

Reference Groups of Ex-Servicemen	Types of Responses (Negative)
1. Young job-seekers intending to get the jobs which ex-servicemen aspire	AGGRESSION
2. Old friends of the same age-group in Civilian employment	DEMORALISATION
3. Old retired civilians leading relatively peaceful life after having fulfilled most of their lifetime responsibilities.	DISSATISFACTION

It can be seen that once an ex-serviceman is confronted with the members of each group, his responses towards them vary. Nevertheless, all the responses are negative in their character and in the process of self-evaluation with the members of these groups he is bound to experience psychological strain. Given the age and added family responsibility he finds himself helpless in making use of such strains to his favour and advantage. He finds himself in great difficulties in taking up the challenge of post-retirement career all alone and look forward to institutions, associations, friends and relatives to extend him helping hands.

No doubt, the ex-servicemen have some sour experiences when they come across persons of their reference group. But they are far better than those placed in various social categories having conditions analogous to the ex-servicemen. One of the main purposes of formulating a typology of re-settlement has been to have a correct appraisal of the problems of ex-Servicemen. The fact that they are placed under 'evenly balanced resettlement' (EBR) category should provide them with some stimulus for self-introspection.

NOTES

1. For a detailed discussion on diagnostic research, see Ramkrishna Mukherjee, *What will it be? Explorations in Inductive Sociology*, New Delhi, 1979, pp. 206-29.
2. The diagnostic research is important and inevitable for prognosis. No prescription for the solution of a problem can be given unless it is well diagnosed. However, without entering into the debate of scope of Sociology, we firmly believe that prognosis of the social problem is as much a concern of Sociology as its diagnosis. The belief not only asserts the fact that there must always be a clear purpose behind a sociological study but also the fact that the one who can grasp and analyse the problem is in a better

position to recommend its solutions.

3. The folk literature of Haryana is full of songs, dances and drama with the soldier or soldier's wife as its main theme. Raja Ram Shastri, *Haryana Ka Lok Sahitya*, 1984, Lok Sampark, Haryana, Chandigarh. Popular Bhojpuri Skit called "*Loha Singh*" by Rameshwar Singh Kashyap can be seen as a cultural response to the chequered and belated military tradition of Bihar.

APPENDIX A

Phone: 3010012

Dte Gen Re-settlement
Ministry of Defence
New Delhi 110 011

No. 2767/DXSM/Emp-3

21 Jul 87

To
Secretaries of all RSBs and all Zonal Directors.

Definition of Ex-serviceman

Reference DGR's telegram of 26 June 87.

2. Definition of ex-serviceman as given in Government of India, Ministry of Personnel, Personal Grievances and Pension's CM No. 36034/5/85/Estt (SCT) of 27 Oct 86 is to be implemented from 01 July 1987. The Ministry has clarified that this definition will only be made applicable to personnel retiring after 01 July, 1987. All ex-defence personnel who had retired prior to that date and e.g. had done only 5 years service or had served for a continuous period of 6 months after attestation and released for reasons other than at their own request, dismissal, discharge will continue to be treated as ex-servicemen.

3. Definition given in the Office Memorandum of 14 April, 1987 therefore is to be read in conjunction with Office Memorandums of 27 Mar., 1987 and 27 Oct., 1986 which have been sent as enclosures with OM of 14 Apr., 1987.

Sd/-
(S.S. Chaudhri)
Commodore
Director (Employment)

No. 36034/5/85-Estt (SCT)
GOVERNMENT OF INDIA
Ministry of Personnel, Public Grievances & Pensions
(Department of Personnel & Training)
New Delhi, the 14th April, 1987

OFFICE MEMORANDUM

Subject: Recommendation No. 15.2 of the High Level Committee on the problems of Ex-servicemen - Revision of the definition of 'Ex-serviceman' in the Ex-servicemen (Re-employment in Central Civil Services and Posts) Rules, 1979.

The undersigned is directed to say that the High Level Committee on the Problems of Ex-servicemen recommended the following definition of the term 'Ex-serviceman':

"An 'ex-serviceman' means a person, who has served in any rank whether as a combatant or non-combatant in the Regular Army, Navy and Air Force of the Indian Union and

(i) who retired from such service after earning his/her pension; or
(ii) who has been released from such service on medical grounds attributable to military service or circumstances beyond his control and awarded medical or other disability pension; or
(iii) who has been released, otherwise than on his own request, from such service as a result of reduction in establishment; or
(iv) who has been released from such service after completing the specific period of

engagements, otherwise than at his own request or by way of dismissal or discharge on account of misconduct or inefficiency, and has been given a gratuity; and includes personnel of the Territorial Army of the following categories, namely:

(a) Pension holders for continuous embodies service
(b) Persons with disability attributable to military service; and
(c) Gallantry award winners."

After careful consideration the Government have opted the above definition recommended by the High Level Committee. However, it may be observed that in the new suggested definition certain categories of personnel which have served in the Armed Forces of the Union have been excluded for consideration as ex-servicemen, whereas certain additional categories of Territorial Army Personnel have been added in the revised definition. The Notification containing the revised definition was issued on 27th October 1986 (see Annexure A), and published in the official Gazette on 15-11-1986. The Notification, gives effect to the new definition from the date of its publication, but since some of the categories were excluded without adequate publicity, the effect of the earlier Notification of 27th October, 1986 has been, stayed by issuing another Notification dated 27-3-87 (copy enclosed as Annexure B) in which the date of effect has been indicated as 1-7-87. The net effect is that the following two categories of personnel, who were included in the pre-revised definition of 'ex-servicemen' will now cease to be treated as ex-servicemen w.e.f. 1-7-87; as will be seen from the following proviso, namely,

"Any person who has been released:

(a) at his own request after completing 5 years' service in the Armed Forces of the Union; or
(b) After serving for a continuous period of six months after attestation, otherwise than at his own request or by way of dismissal or discharge on account of mis-conduct or inefficiency or has been transferred to the reserve pending such release;

shall also deemed to be an ex-serviceman for the purposes of this clause."

3. The Territorial Army Personnel will however be treated as ex-servicemen w.e.f. 15-11-86.

4. Ministry of Finance etc., are, therefore, requested to bring the contents of this Office Memorandum to the notice of all the appointing authorities under their administrative control and ensure that there is no laxity on the part of the authorities implementing the above instructions.

Sd/-
(Bata K. Dey)
Director (JCA)

ANNEXURE A

No. 36034/5/85-Estt (SCT)

GOVERNMENT OF INDIA

Ministry of Personnel, P.G. & Pensions

(Department of Personnel & Training)

New Delhi, the 27th October, 1986

NOTIFICATION

GSR :- In exercise of the powers conferred by the proviso to article 309 of the Constitution, the President hereby makes the following rules further to amend the Ex-Servicemen (Re-employment in Central Civil Services and Posts) Rules, 1979 namely:—

1.(1) These rules may be called the Ex-Servicemen (Re-employment in Central Civil Services and Posts) Amendment Rules, 1986.

(2) They shall come into force on the date of their publication in the Official Gazette.

2. In rule 2 of the Ex-servicemen (Re-employment in Central Civil Services and Posts) Rules, 1979 for clause (c) the following clause shall be substituted, namely:—

(c) 'ex-serviceman' means a person, who has served in any rank (whether as a combatant or as a non-combatant) in the Regular Army, Navy and Air Force of the Indian Union but does not include a person who has served in the Defence Security Corps, the General Reserve Engineering Force, the Lok Sahayak Sena and the Para Military Forces; and

(i) who has retired from such service after earning his/her pension; or

(ii) who has been released from such service on medical grounds attributable to military service or circumstances beyond his control and awarded medical or other disability pension; or

(iii) who has been released, otherwise than on his own request, from such service as a result of reduction in establishment; or

(iv) who has been released from such service after completing the specific period of engagement otherwise than at his own request or by way of dismissal or discharge on account of misconduct or inefficiency, and has been given a gratuity; and includes personnel of the Territorial Army of the following categories, namely:

(a) Pension holders for continuous *embodied* service;

(b) persons with disability attributable to military service; and

(c) gallantry award winners.

Explanation: The persons serving in the Armed Forces of the Union, who on retirement from service, would come under the category of 'ex-servicemen', may be permitted to apply for re-employment *one year* before the completion of the specified terms of engagement and avail themselves of all concessions available to ex-servicemen but shall not be permitted to leave the uniform until they complete the specified term of engagement in the Armed Forces of the Union.

Note: The principal rules were published *vide* notification No. GSR 1530, dated 29th Dec., 1979 in the *Gazette of India*, Part-II, Section 3, Sub-section (1) at pages 3004-3005.

(Sd/-) BATA K. DEY, Director (JCA)

ANNEXURE B

No. 36034/5/85-Estt (SCT)

GOVERNMENT OF INDIA
Ministry of Personnel, P.G. & Pensions
(Department of Personnel & Training)
New Delhi, the 27th March 1987

NOTIFICATION

GSR :- In exercise of the powers conferred by the proviso to article 309 of the Constitution, the President hereby makes the following rules further to amend the Ex-Servicemen (Re-employment in Central Civil Services and Posts) Rules, 1979, namely:—

1. (1) These rules may be called the Ex-Servicemen (Re-employment in Central Civil Services and Posts) Amendment Rules, 1987.

   (2) They shall be deemed to have come into force on the 15th day of Nov., 1986.

2. In rule 2 of the Ex-servicemen (Re-employment in Central Civil Services and Posts) Rules, 1979, to clause (c), the following proviso shall be added, namely:

"Provided that for the period commencing on the 15th day of Nov., 1986 and ending with the 30th day of June, 1987, any person who has been released:–

(a) at his own request after completing 5 years' service in the Armed Forces of the Union; or

(b) after serving for a continuous period of six months after attestation, otherwise than at his own request or by way of dismissal or discharge on account of mis-conduct or in-efficiency or has been transferred to the reserve pending such release;

shall also deemed to be an Ex-serviceman for the purpose for this clause."

Note: Principal rules were published *vide* Notification No. GSR 1530 dated the 29th Dec., 1979 and subsequently amended *vide* Notification No. GSR-973 dated the 15th Nov., 1986 in the *Gazette of India*, Part-II Section-3, Sub-Section (1)

(Sd/-)
BATA K. DEY, Director (JCA)

BIBLIOGRAPHY

Government of India Publications

A Guide to Resettlement of Ex-Servicemen, 1984, DGR, G.O.I.

Equation of Service Trades with Civil Trades, (Undated), DGR, G.O.I.

Ex-Servicemen as entrepreneur, 1982, DGR, G.O.I.

A Handbook of Resettlement Training of Ex-Servicemen, 1984, 1982, DGR, G.O.I.

A Handbook of Self-Employment of Ex-Servicemen, 1984, DGR, G.O.I.

Kya Aur Kaise? Bhutpurva O.R. Evam J.C.O., Ko Punarvas Mein Sahayata, (In Hindi) 1982, DGR, G.O.I.

Preparing Ex-Servicemen for Self-Employment, 1986, DGR, G.O.I.

Report of the High Level Committee on Problems of Ex-Servicemen, 1984, Ministry of Defence, G.O.I.

SEMFEX SCHEME (Self-Employment for Ex-Servicemen), 1987, DGR, G.O.I.

Your Tomorrow, Would you like to prepare for it? 1981, DGR, G.O.I.

Books and Articles

Ashraf, Kunwar Muhammad, *Life and Conditions of the People of Hindustan*, Munshiram Manoharlal, New Delhi, 1970.

Athar Ali, M., *The Mughal Nobility Under Aurangzeb*, Asia Publishing House, New Delhi, 1970.

Heraud, Brian J., *Sociology and Social Work: Perspectives and Problems* 1970 (Pergamon Press, Oxford, 1970).

Majumdar, Bimal Kanti, *The Military System in Ancient India*, Firma K.L. Mukhopadhyay, Calcutta 1960.

Mukherjee, Ramakrishna, *What Will It Be? Explorations in Inductive Sociology*, New Delhi, 1979.

Oommen, T.K., "The Concept of Dominant Caste", *Contributions to Indian Sociology*, New Series, Vol. IV, Dec., 1970, pp. 73-83.

———, "Insiders and Outsiders in India: Primordial Collectivitism and Cultural Pluralism in National Building", *International Sociology*, Vol. 1, No. 1, University College of Cardiff Press, Bristol, 1986.

———, *Professional Social Work - As I See It*, Department of Social Work, Jamia Millia Islamia, New Delhi, 1987.

Sachchidananda, "Caste and Conflict in a Bihar Village", *Eastern Anthropologist*, vol. XX, No. 11, May-Aug. 1967, Deptt. of Anthropology, Lucknow University.

———, *The Changing Munda*, Concept Publishing Company, New Delhi, 1979.

Saksena, K.M.L., *The Military System of India (1850-1900)*, Sterling Publishers Pvt. Ltd., New Delhi, 1974.

Sarkar, Jagdish Narayan, *The Art of War in Medieval India*, Munshiram Manoharlal Publishers Pvt. Ltd., New Delhi, 1984.

Satyendra Kishore *National Integration in India*, Sterling Publishers, Pvt. Ltd., 1987.

Sharma, O.P., *Military Law in India*, N.M. Tripathi Pvt. Ltd., Bombay, 1973.

Shastri, Raja Ram, *Haryana Ka Lok Sahitya*, (In Hindi and Haryanvi) Lok Sampark, Haryana, 1984.

Singh, Major Madan Paul, *Indian Army under the East India Company*, Sterling Publishers Pvt. Ltd., New Delhi, 1976.

Singh, M.K., *Resettlement Problems of Retired Army Officers*, Mittal Publishers, New Delhi, 1985.

Srinivas, M.N., "The Dominant Caste in Rampura", *American Anthropologist*, February, 1959.

Vidyarthi, Avinash Chandra (ed.), *Bhikhari Thakur Granthawali* Part-I, (In Hindi and Bhojpuri) Lok Kalakar Bhikhari Thakur Ashram, Qutabpur (Saran), Bihar, 1979.

Watson, G.R., *The Roman Soldier*, Thames & Hudson, Bristol, 1969.

Yogendra Singh, *Modernisation of Indian Traditions*, Thompson Press, New Delhi, 1973.

Journals and Magazines

The USI Journal, A Monthly Journal of United Services Institution, Kashmir House, New Delhi.

Indian Ex-Servicemen (Monthly Publication of the Indian Ex-Services League), New Delhi.

Sainik Punarvas, DGR, G.O.I., New Delhi.

INDEX